MW01156437

ALSO BY MARVIN CARLSON

André Antoine's Memories of the Théâtre-Libre
The Theatre of the French Revolution
The French Stage in the Nineteenth Century
The German Stage in the Nineteenth Century
Goethe and the Weimar Theatre
The Italian Stage from Goldoni to D'Annunzio
Theories of the Theatre
The Italian Shakesperians

PLACES OF PERFORMANCE

PLACES OF

Cornell University Press   ITHACA AND LONDO

PERFORMANCE

The Semiotics of Theatre Architecture

MARVIN CARLSON

First published 1989 by Cornell University Press
First printing, Cornell Paperbacks, 1993

An earlier version of the material in Chapter 3 appeared in *Theatre Journal*, 40 (March 1988) under the title "The Theatre as Civic Monument."

Printed in the United States of America

Library of Congress Cataloging-in-Publication Data

Carlson, Marvin A., 1935–
    Places of performance : the semiotics of theatre architecture /
Marvin Carlson.
        p.   cm.
    Includes index.
    ISBN 978-0-8014-8094-2 (pbk. : alk. paper)

    1. Theaters—Construction. 2. Signs and symbols in architecture.
3. Architecture—Psychological aspects. I. Title.
NA6821.C36 1989   725'.822—dc19   88-47936

Cornell University Press strives to use environmentally responsible suppliers and materials to the fullest extent possible in the publishing of its books. Such materials include vegetable-based, low-VOC inks and acid-free papers that are recycled, totally chlorine-free, or partly composed of non-wood fibers. For further information, visit our website at www.cornellpress.cornell.edu.

Paperback printing: 10 9 8 7 6

To Tom Sebeok,
friend and inspiration

Contents

PLACES OF PERFORMANCE

The belief and manners of all people are embodied in the edifices they raised.

—A. Welby Pugin

In all times, the architect has been the interpreter and the historian of human kind.

—César Daly

How Do Theatres Mean?

Brander Matthews, the first American professor to hold an appointment in theatre studies and a pioneer in the development of theatre history as a discipline, engaged in a lengthy and famous debate with his colleague at Columbia University, English professor Joel Spingarn, upon the usefulness of the study of the physical spaces in which historical dramas were performed. Matthews insisted that a proper understanding of the plays of Shakespeare, Sophocles, Molière, or Ibsen required a knowledge of what sort of physical stage each had in mind as he was creating his dramas, and to this end developed for students a collection of models of historical theatres which still may be seen at Columbia. Spingarn, championing what he called "new criticism," which attempted to analyze the written text without the "distractions" of cultural or historical context, naturally deplored Matthews's interest in such matters. The study of the history of theatrical spaces, he once observed, had no more to do with the understanding of the drama than the study of the history of printing had to do with the understanding of poetry.

Spingarn's position boasts few adherents today, even in the most conservative departments of English, and the study of the physical conditions of performance has long been generally accepted as a legitimate, indeed essential part of the historical study of both drama and theatre. Nevertheless, this study has remained rather narrowly focused, a result of the particular concerns of the tradition shared by Spingarn and Matthews, which was strongly oriented toward the written text and especially the established classic. Though their methods differed, their goal was the same: to gain a better understanding of why Shakespeare, for example, wrote the plays he did in the way he did.

With such a concern, Matthews and subsequent theatre historians have tended, not surprisingly, to devote most of their attention to that part of the performance space where the play is enacted—the stage, its entrances and exits, its size and shape, its scenery and illumination. As one moved further and further from the stage, the interest of historians accordingly lessened—so that the auditorium received less attention, the lobbies and other public areas less still, the external appearance and physical surroundings of the theatre practically none at all.

In recent years, however, as we have come to consider the theatre experience in new ways, this model and this procedure have become increasingly inadequate. No longer do we necessarily approach theatre primarily as the physical enactment of a written text with our historical concern anchored in the interplay between that text and its physical realization. We are now at least equally likely to look at the theatre experience in a more global way, as a sociocultural event whose meanings and interpretations are not to be sought exclusively in the text being performed but in the experience of the audience assembled to share in the creation of the total event.

Such a change of focus requires also a change in the way we look at the places where theatrical performance occurs, which may or may not be traditional theatre buildings. The way an audience experiences and interprets a play, we now recognize, is by no means governed solely by what happens on the stage. The entire theatre, its audience arrangements, its other public spaces, its physical appearance, even its location within a city, are all important elements of the process by which an audience makes meaning of its experience.

The present book seeks to explore some of the implications of these more neglected aspects of the physical surroundings of performance, by way of demonstrating not only how such surroundings reflect the social and cultural concerns and suppositions of their creators and their audiences, but even more important, how they may serve to stimulate or to reinforce within audiences certain ideas of what theatre represents within their society and how the performances it is offering are to be interpreted and integrated into the rest of their social and cultural life. We will, in short, be considering how places of performance generate social and cultural meanings of their own which in turn help to structure the meaning of the entire theatre experience.

Although this inquiry will be oriented toward specific historical illustration rather than theoretical discussion, the methods of analysis will be based upon strategies derived from and suggested by modern semiotic theory, since semiotics is concerned with precisely the sort of question we seek to explore—the processes by which any cultural artefact, such as a theatre building, is given a meaning or meanings by its society. This opening chapter will provide a brief overview of those elements of semiotic theory, a very small part of this vast field, which seem most relevant to the discussion at hand. At present, the strategies suggested by this way of looking at cultural manifestations seem to me to offer the best available tools for analyzing how theatres mean and how their meanings relate to the audience's understanding and experience of the theatre event.

The fact that every human child is born into a preexisting society and culture means that practically from the moment of birth the child must engage in a continuing relationship with that culture. The methods by which a child learns a language—or a culture—will doubtless long remain a major challenge for psychological researchers, but it is clear that despite the amazing human ability to assimilate the elaborate structures of society, no specific structural systems, linguistic or cultural, may be claimed as innate. Any newborn child, placed in the proper environment, will learn a European, an Asian, or an African language or culture with equal ease.

Children must learn to "speak" a culture as well as a language, to structure the world mentally according to the rules of the society in which they find themselves. This process continues throughout life. It can never reach closure because no culture is itself completely closed and set, nor does any individual continue to relate to surroundings in a permanently fixed way. Nevertheless, we are apparently programmed to "make sense" of our environment, and every culture may be seen on its most fundamental level as a construction to respond to that need. Despite its openness, our continuing interaction with culture provides us with tools for making sense of whatever we see, experience, or think about. Both the hypothetical and tentative interpretations of these data and the processes by which we test and eventually accept or reject them are developed within the structures of meanings provided for us by our culture.

The ubiquity of meaning-making in human society explains why semiotics, the study of how phenomena in the world are related to meaning by humanity, has cast its net so widely among so many hitherto separate disciplines, a process not surprisingly viewed as a sort of doctrinal imperialism by those suspicious of semiotic strategies and procedure. Yet the possibility, indeed the necessity, of so broad a territorial claim by semiotics makes it potentially an extremely valuable approach in a field such as theatre studies. Here the object of investigation is itself so complex and multifaceted that an overarching approach such as that semiotics offers may provide new insights not only into traditional areas of research but, perhaps even more important, into the connections and relationships between those areas.

Only a small part of this potential has so far been explored. Although the combined writings of the Prague School in the 1930s and the revival of interest in semiotic studies in recent years have produced by now a fairly substantial body of writings on theatre subjects,[1] these writings have been for the most part rather traditional in focus, if not in methodology. As a rule, they have applied the strategies of semiotic analysis to already established areas of theoretical investigation in the theatre, and thus have not yet fully taken advantage of other areas to which semiotics could be as readily and perhaps even more profitably applied. The vast majority of modern semiotic analyses of theatre have been concerned primarily (and often exclusively) with the written text, a natural result of the literary and linguistic background of the theorists involved.

The Prague circle, a number of whose members were practicing theatre critics as well as theorists, tended to take a more performance-oriented approach, concentrating on what actually happened on the stage. This sort of concern has recently become more common in semiotic studies, and since about 1980 much greater attention has begun to be paid to the "pragmatic" aspect of theatre and to the contribution of the spectator. Some writers have related this shift to a corresponding shift among theorists from a Saussurian sign model based on the work of Swiss linguist Ferdinand de Saussure, uniting signifier with signified (which would place emphasis on the text or the performance as a sign-producing mechanism) to a model drawn from the American linguist Charles Peirce, who added a third element, the interpretant, thus placing greater emphasis upon the reception of the sign.[2]

As a result, the working methods of a semiotic analysis of the written text, of the performance text, and of the relationship between the two have by now been fairly well established, and the relationship of the audience to both has received significant, though so far less extensive, attention. These areas of investigation will likely and not unreasonably remain the major concern of future semiotic studies of the theatre, but if they remain the exclusive areas of concern, we will not be availing ourselves of the full usefulness of semiotic analysis, which can potentially provide us with a much more global view of the theatrical event.

[1]Kier Elam provides an extensive bibliography in *The Semiotics of Theatre and Drama* (London, 1980).

[2]See, for example, Achim Eschbach, *Pragmasemiotik und Theater* (Tübingen, 1979), 146.

As early as 1943 Eric Buyssens in the pioneering study *Les langages et le discours* suggested that an operatic performance was perhaps the richest object available for semiotic analysis in the culture, because it involved the meanings of words, music, gesture, dance, costumes, scenery, lighting, audience reactions, social relationships, and even the personnel of the theatre—the ushers, the firemen, the police. Buyssens observed that a comprehensive semiotic study of such a phenomenon would have to consider the communication that takes place for a few hours within "an entire world."[3]

Given the complexity of this task, it is hardly surprising that neither Buyssens nor any subsequent semiotician has attempted such an analysis, but it does seem odd that this early observation has left so slight a mark on subsequent theory. It has been not the semioticians, but the theatre theorists influenced by anthropological and sociological concerns who have pointed out that the text-performance-audience interaction should not be considered in a vacuum, but rather as an event embedded in a complex matrix of social concerns and actions, all of which "communicate" or contribute to giving the theatre experience its particular "meaning" to its participants.[4]

Semiotics, however, has an enormous potential for aiding in this more general understanding of theatre not merely as a performed text but as an event embedded in society and culture, involved with meanings on many levels other than those of the text and staging themselves. Clearly, as Buyssens suggested, every element of the spectator's environment during an operatic performance—the singing, the scenery, the orchestra, the lobbies and bars at intermission, the programs, the ushers, the other audience members—contributes to the way in which that spectator "makes sense" of the event, and all these may be subjected to semiotic analysis.

But one may extend Buyssens's suggested analysis still further in the directions suggested by event analysis. Obviously the meaning of an event depends to some extent upon its context, the way in which it is related to other events and to a cultural milieu. The study of this dimension of the theatre experience necessarily takes us outside even Buyssens's "entire world" exisiting for a few hours within the confines of the opera house to consider such matters as the relation of a visit to the opera to the rest of life—how it fits into the social routine, where the opera house is located in the urban plan and how one arrives there,

---

[3]Eric Buyssens, *Les langages et le discours* (Brussels, 1943), 56. All translations are my own unless otherwise identified.

[4]See, for example, Richard Schechner, "Towards a Poetics of Performance," in *Essays on Performance Theory* (New York, 1977), 108–39.

what preparations must be made for the operatic event on the part of the public or on that of the performers and management, and so on. The range of potential investigation is indeed daunting, but it is liberating as well. Although semiotics has not so far fulfilled this function to any considerable degree, it has the potential to encourage theatre scholars to look beyond the confines of traditional theatre studies, which have tended to regard theatre texts and theatre events as isolated phenomena related, if to anything, primarily to other texts and events within the theatre, and to see theatre as a cultural phenomenon with many more operative dimensions of meaning.

The present book considers only one area within this broad field of potential investigation, but it is an area that has as yet received almost no attention from theatre semioticians—the building or space in which theatre takes place and its contributions to the meaning-structure of the theatre event as a whole. A permanently or temporarily created ludic space, a ground for the encounter of spectator and performer, is a phenomenon found in a wide variety of societies and historical periods, but like any such phenomenon, can carry an almost infinite variety of special meanings according to the usages of those societies.

Normally when we think of theatrical performance we imagine it taking place within an architectural space designed for that purpose, although history and quite likely our own experience can provide us with examples of theatre taking place in other sorts of locations as well. We shall begin with this most unconventional sort of theatrical space, considering some of the reasons for theatre to be located outside its own distinct building and some of the ways in which this seeming disadvantage has been utilized to deepen and enrich the message of the theatre event as a whole.

The major part of this book, however, will naturally be concerned with specific architectural spaces created for theatrical use and with the play of meanings involved in them. The theatre is in fact one of the most persistant architectural objects in the history of Western culture. Martin Krampen, in *Meaning in the Urban Environment*, observes that as "urban ideologies" change, the meaning of the urban environment as a whole changes as well, a change reflected in what Krampen calls the "repertory of architectural objects." New normative types such as factories or railway stations replace abandoned types such as palaces or triumphal arches, representing not only new urban activities but entire new social organizations.[5]

[5]Martin Krampen, *Meaning in the Urban Environment* (London, 1979), 69.

Krampen does not remark, however, on those normative types that remain a part of the urban environment over long periods of time as others come and go, adjusting in some manner to major shifts in ideologies and thus providing particularly interesting examples of shifting meanings in the urban text. A major example of such a type is the theatre, which throughout the classical period and from the Renaissance onward has been among the most generally found architectural elements appearing in the various normative lists of such objects. Thus we find theatres listed among the "utilitarian" public buildings, along with markets and baths, in Vitruvius' *Ten Books of Architecture*, a standard reference for Renaissance architects. Subsequent normative lists such as L. B. Alberti's *Ten Books on Architecture* (1755) and J. N. L. Durand's *Précis des leçons d'architecture* (1817) added to or reduced Vitruvius' list, but theatres remained one of the few constants and would doubtless be included were such a list to be drawn up today. The other shifts in such lists, however, provide clear evidence that the public image of what makes up a city is changing, and the stability of theatre as an element does not mean that its urban role is stable but, on the contrary, that it has been able to accommodate itself to a variety of urban functions as the city around it has changed.

One of the first works to attempt an application of semiotic analysis to architecture was Umberto Eco's *La struttura assente* in 1968. Here Eco suggested that a specific architectural object might be considered a sign and, like any sign is a duality composed of a meaning (a signified) and something created by a culture to stand for that meaning (a signifier). In this case the signifier is the architectural object (a church, a house, a store), tied by cultural codes to its function (a space for worship, for dwelling, for trade). Were we to apply this analysis to a historical theatre structure, we could say that the signified was the space for the encounter of spectator and actor and that the building itself, associated by the culture with this encounter, was the signifier.

If the cultural meaning of a building were restricted to this level, its semiotic would be quickly and simply described, but as Eco and others have noted, almost any sign, once created, has a tendency to become the signifier for new signifieds, by taking on new semantic overtones beyond the original. The first or what we might call the "functional" level might be thought of as the denotative, and the further levels built upon it connotative, but Eco argues that such terms as "utility" and "function" should not be confined to the denotative aspects of an object. A royal throne serves the "function" of any chair—to be sat upon—but it also has other and more important functions based upon its connotations. Thus Eco prefers to speak of primary and secondary levels of meaning. Houses and churches are dwellings and places of worship on their primary level, but they provide a host of secondary meanings as well, signifying a great deal about the way their users relate to society as a whole both immediately and historically.

Clearly the same observation may be made of the theatre building, which in addition to providing a space for the performance of a dramatic text has taken on a wide variety of social meanings over the centuries—a cultural monument, a site of display for a dominant social class, an emblem of depravity and vice, a center of political activism, a haven of retreat from the world of harsh reality. Nor are these many connotations without effect on the physical theatre space; many elements, some evident, others subtle, of contemporary and historical theatres provide striking evidence of the semiotic role played by a theatre in its society.

A strategy for the analysis of such elements is suggested in Roland Barthes's *Elements of Semiology*, a work that in turn draws heavily, as does Eco, upon the linguistic analysis of Ferdinand de Saussure. Saussure speaks of two basic types of relationships between linguistic elements, based on two different mental activities, both of which contribute to the creation of meaning. These are usually referred to in modern semiotic theory as syntagmatic and paradigmatic (or systematic) relationships. If we consider the meaning of a word in a sentence, the first of these analyzes the word as an element in that linear sequence, how it relates to the surrounding elements. The second considers the relationships between this word and the many rejected alternatives which its presence may evoke in the mind but which do not form part of the utterance itself, such as synonyms, antonyms, homonyms, and so on. Of particular interest in the light of our present discussion, Saussure illustrates this distinction with an architectural metaphor:

> From this double point of view, a linguistic unity is comparable to a specific part of a building, a column for example; on the one hand this has a certain relationship with the architrave that it supports. This connection of two units, both present in space, suggests the syntagmatic relationship. On the other hand, if this column is of the Doric order it evokes a mental comparison with other orders (Ionic, Corinthian, etc.) which are elements not present. This relationship is associative [paradigmatic].[6]

Barthes suggests a slightly different way of applying these two axes to

[6]Ferdinand de Saussure, *Cours de linguistique générale* (Paris, 1916), 171.

architectural analysis, by considering not only single architectural elements such as columns, but spatial divisions as well. His syntagmatic axes would consider "the sequence of the details at the level of the whole building," while the paradigmatic would deal with "the variations of style of a single element in a building, various types of roof, balcony, hall, etc."[7]

Although architectural analyses along these general lines have been undertaken, there has been as yet no attempt to apply such a strategy specifically to theatrical structures. Certain syntagmatic relationships (such as that of stage to orchestra or to proscenium arch) have been given considerable attention in conventional historical studies, as have certain paradigmatic ones (thrust versus proscenium stages, for example), but others, especially those involving parts of the theatre not actually utilized in performance, have been virtually ignored. A semiotic approach to theatre architecture should encourage us to look not only at the traditional elements of stage and auditorium but at every distinct element of the theatre complex for what it may reveal about the meanings of this building for its society. Ideally, such analysis should be not only synchronic (considering the relationship between elements at a particular time) but also diachronic (considering temporal changes in elements or in the connotations of elements), since the meanings of those elements that make up a theatre structure, and sometimes the elements themselves, will change as the society that interprets them changes. The appearance, development, and decline of boxes in theatre auditoriums is closely tied to a whole system of social values, which we shall at least briefly examine. The same cartouche with fleurs-de-lys over the proscenium of the theatre at Versailles had obviously a very different meaning to the original audiences who attended that theatre than it does to the tourists who visit it today. The two most general ways of looking at the components of a building and their interrelationships in terms of social and cultural messages are through the articulation of space and through the choice of visual, decorative elements, and we shall give attention to each of these in turn.

The syntagmatic and paradigmatic axes themselves must not be confined to a single level of semiotic analysis, but may be considered operative wherever cultural codes allow a phenomenon to be analyzed by means of subelements arranged in a meaningful order but theoretically replaceable by other elements. Thus one may, as Barthes

[7]Roland Barthes, *Elements of Semiology*, trans. Annette Lavers and Colin Smith (New York, 1968), 63.

suggests, consider the implications of different varieties of hall within the total articulation of a building, just as one can on a different level, consider, as Saussure suggests, the implications of different styles of column within the total articulation of a hall.

One may also move to a more comprehensive level, regarding the theatre building itself as a single unit variable paradigmatically within the larger structure of the theatre's urban district or of the city as a whole. This latter aspect of the physical theatre is another to which theatre historians have given comparatively little attention. It is generally known, of course, that public theatres in Shakespeare's time were located on the fringes of the city in rather questionable neighborhoods, and the terms "Broadway," "off-Broadway theatre," "West End theatres," and "Boulevard theatres" conjure up at least vague images of buildings associated with certain geographical areas, but for the majority of major theatres in most historical periods our mental image of their interior or the reproduction of that interior in our standard histories is rarely matched by the slightest idea of where within the city that theatre was located or what that location may have meant to audiences of the time. And yet surely this is a critical part of our understanding of how these audiences viewed and interacted with that theatre.

Merely establishing the exact physical location of a historic theatre, though this is often no small task, is of course only the first step in analysis. Then comes the usually much more difficult task of gaining some understanding of the cultural and social significance of that location. Fortunately some tools for this task are already at hand. Just as the strategies of architectural semiotics suggest techniques for dealing with the elements of the theatre building as a total structure, so the closely related field of urban semiotics, though it is at this point much less developed, can provide some assistance in analyzing the theatre in its larger context.

Certain of the concerns and approaches of urban semiotics were anticipated in Kenneth Lynch's fascinating 1960 book, *The Image of the City*. Lynch begins with the observation that "structuring and identifying the environment is a vital ability among all mobile animals," and proceeds to examine the methods by which the inhabitants of a city intellectually structure their surroundings.[8] He sees the mental "image" of a city as built up from a composite of five types of elements—paths, which are the learned routes by which inhabitants

[8]Kenneth Lynch, *The Image of the City* (Cambridge, Mass., 1960), 3.

move from one part of the city to another; nodes, where two or more paths intersect; districts, which are relatively large areas with some common characteristics; edges, which act as barriers to paths and as boundaries to districts; and landmarks, which are striking urban elements used for orientation. Each of these has important implications for the placement of theatres within a city. At certain times theatres themselves have served as urban landmarks, as we may see in the theatres of imperial Rome or in the baroque opera house, or have located themselves near landmarks or nodes (such as Times Square or Piccadilly Circus) to increase their visibility and ease of access. Perhaps most interesting is the relationship of theatres to particular districts. Often, of course, theatres tend to cluster together in an "entertainment" district, but they may also be found in a great variety of other urban locations, and the location will inevitably condition the public image of the building. Even the "entertainment" district may vary a good deal in its connotations from one city to another.

In two papers on semiology and urbanism, Barthes has outlined if not a methodology, at least a theoretical approach to urban semiotics, drawing in part on Lynch's work.[9] A "semiotic of the city" should view the city as a "text" created by human beings in space, spoken by and speaking to those who inhabit it, move through it, and observe it. An analysis of this text could be undertaken by structuralist methods, that is, by a study of the opposition, alternation, and juxtaposition of the elements within it. Barthes calls particular attention to the center of the city as an area charged with signification, a "ludic space" where the most concentrated encounters between inhabitants occur, and where, of course, theatres have often tended to gather.

French sociologists Sylvia Ostrowetsky and Richard Fauqué have suggested strategies for pursuing the sort of urban analysis Barthes proposes.[10] Ostrowetsky proposed a consideration of urban semiotics on three levels: "morphemes," the individual elements of a building such as doors, windows, and decoration; architectural "signs," such as a single building; and "urbemes," higher integrated units such as a street composed of aligned shops converging on a monument. Both she and Fauqué believe that the "meanings" of elements on each of these

[9]Barthes, "Semiologie e urbanistica," *Selezione della critica d'arte contemporana* 10 (1967), 7–17, and "Sémiologie et urbanisme," *Architecture d'aujourd'hui* 153 (1971), 11–13.
[10]Sylvia Ostrowetsky, "De l'urbain à l'urbain," *Cahiers internationales de sociologie* 52–53 (Jan.–June 1972), 108–9, and Richard Fauqué, "Pour une nouvelle approche sémiologique à la ville," *Espaces et sociétés* 9 (July 1973), 23–26.

levels are based on opposition and context. To take obvious examples, larger and higher urban elements tend to suggest value and power, as do central versus peripheral locations within districts.

Certainly these three levels can be applied to a study of what meanings theatre buildings have had or might have to the inhabitants of the cities where they are located. Both the interior and the exterior of a theatre building are composed of decorative and structural elements that may be read in terms of architectural, linguistic, mythological, or design codes developed in a rich and suggestive pattern of opposition and juxtaposition with other such elements in other theatres and in other urban structures. The appearance of a theatre building as a whole and its similarity to or difference from other urban elements provide a second level of analysis, and a third is available in the theatre's enclosing "urbeme"—its immediately related surroundings. Ostrowetsky notes that the same tower will have quite a different meaning when it is located at an urban center from what it would have in a suburb. Clearly the same thing is true of a theatre. Where it is built will say a great deal about what view of theatre its builders have and how it will be regarded by the public.

Another Barthes essay, "The Eiffel Tower," suggests how these district connotations operate in an analysis of Paris. Every visitor to the tower, Barthes says, makes a semiotic or structuralist analysis of the city without knowing it. "He spontaneously distinguishes separate—because known—points, and yet does not stop linking them, perceiving them within a great functional space; in short, he separates and groups; Paris offers itself to him as an object virtually *prepared*, exposed to the intelligence, but which he must himself construct by a formal activity of the mind."[11] The physical panorama thus calls into consciousness the mental map Lynch described and challenges the individual to "make sense" of the view before him by means of that organization of districts, landmarks, and so on, a process Barthes called "decipherment." Most important, this process is not simply one of identification of physical relationships, but also the recall of previously established functional and connotative ones, as Barthes suggests: "on the great polar axis, perpendicular to the horizontal curve of the river, three zones stacked one after the other, as though along a prone body, three functions of human life; at the top, at the foot of Montmartre, pleasure; at the center, around the Opéra, materiality, business, commerce; toward the bottom, at the foot of the Panthéon,

[11]Barthes, *The Eiffel Tower and Other Mythologies,* trans. Richard Howard (New York, 1979), 9–10.

knowledge, study; then, to the right and left, enveloping this vital axis like two protective muffs, two large zones of habitation, one residential, the other blue-collar."[12]

The location of theatres within the Parisian text reflects these rough connotative divisions with perfect accuracy. In the Montmartre "pleasure" district we find clustered the cabarets and music halls, around the "materiality and commerce" center not only the Opéra, but most of the major commercial theatres, and around the Panthéon "knowledge and study" center the Odéon and small experimental and avantgarde theatres. Few theatres of course are to be found in the two "habitation" zones, though the blue-collar connotations of one of them has resulted in recent years in the project of placing there a new "people's" opera.

The pages that follow will draw upon strategies suggested by these and other theorists interested in exploring the meanings of architectural and urban structures to examine some of the history of the Western theatre in a fresh way, to suggest how the space of performance may contribute to the meaning of the total theatrical experience. Theatre is not always, of course, produced in buildings designed particularly for that purpose, and we shall begin with some consideration of how nontheatrical performance spaces may contribute to the total theatre experience, looking first at theatrical utilization of other public urban spaces, and then at the utilization of spaces less accessible to the general public. We shall then turn to the more familiar cases of structures designed for theatrical performance, considering first the free-standing or monumental theatre, the most common form of national theatres, then the theatre in a facade row, the most common form of modern commercial theatre. Finally we shall move inside these structures to consider some of the connotations of spatial arrangements and selection of decorative elements. In this way we shall gain some idea of how at least one important segment of the "entire world" of the theatre event—its physical surroundings, studied at each of Ostrowetsky's levels—relates to the manner in which the public interprets that theatrical event.

[12]Ibid., 12-13.

I

The City as Theatre

The late Middle Ages and early Renaissance constitute the major historical period when theatre existed as an important part of urban life without any specific architectural element being devoted to its exclusive use. The absence of a specifically theatrical structure from the medieval city's repertory of architectural objects by no means indicates that the physical situation of theatre performance within the city was devoid of symbolic significance. On the contrary, a situation allowing those producing a performance to place it in whatever locale seemed most suitable meant that theatre could use to its own advantage the already existing connotations of other spaces both in themselves and in their placement within the city, and this was in fact consistently done. Such a dynamic was particularly congenial to the medieval world view, which delighted in the discovery of correspondences and in building rich symbolic structures by relating various systems of signs to each other.

The symbolic center of the medieval town was the cathedral, and nowhere else in the city was so rich a trove of symbolic referents concentrated. A famous passage in Hugo's *Notre Dame de Paris* considers the cathedral as the central repository of signs for its culture. Legend, allegory, doctrine, the whole sum of medieval knowledge of the world, divine and human, was here represented in painting, sculpture, stained glass, and space. At the same time this fabric of symbols, rich as it was, also served as a setting, a container for the even more central symbolic systems of the performed rituals of the church, by which the citizens of the city were led to a direct participation in the divine mysteries.

The liturgical drama that grew up within the cathedral occupied a position somewhere between religious ritual and the rich cadre of architecture, sculpture, and stained glass which enclosed that ritual, and drew upon the symbolic potential of each. Carol Heinz has documented the close connection between the massive west fronts that appeared during the Carolingian period and the architectural and iconographic symbols of death and resurrection of the time. As the common theme of portals in the western facade, the last judgment also came to be associated with this area, as did baptism (the symbolic death and resurrection of the penitent sinner).[1] An altar to the Savior was often placed here in relation to these events. It is in this part of the cathedral, already rich with appropriate associations, that Heinz suggests the first liturgical Easter plays were presented. The more traditional view has placed these performances near the high altar, with the crypt beneath serving as an icon for the tomb.[2] Whichever view is correct, historians agree that the new dramatic presentation built upon the connotations already present in a space created for nondramatic purposes.

Gradually liturgical performances came to utilize other parts of the cathedral, and the same dynamic continued. The cathedral itself was architecturally oriented with the presumed world axes, the main line running east and west, with a lesser north-south crossing. To the east lay Jerusalem and the presumed site of the lost Eden, and the celebrant entering the cathedral moved in this direction to reach the high altar. The path of church processions, east toward the high altar or west toward the altar of the Savior, already evocative of world or cosmic journeys, were in turn echoed by movements along these same axes in the liturgical dramas—the journey to Emmaus, the race of the disciples to the tomb, the journey of the Magi.

The tripartite division of the cathedral east-center-west into choir, nave, and narthex provided a supplementary spatial orientation. Between the altar of the Savior, with its evocation of the passion, the resurrection, and the last judgment, and the eastern altar of the Virgin, suggesting the nativity and the church itself, the middle of the nave or the crossing of the transepts provided a less heavily charged religious space, the space not only of processions toward one end of the church or the other, but of more "earthly" locations required by the liturgical dramas. Thus the Rouen "Jeu des pèlerins d'Emmaus" places the "castelli Emmaus" in the middle of the nave, the Bilsen "Office de l'étoile" there situates the "palace" of Herod, and the Rouen "Pro-

---

[1]Carol Heinz, *Recherches sur les rapports entre l'architecture et la liturgie à l'époque carolingienne* (Paris, 1963), 140, 164.

[2]For a comparison of these views, see Elie Konigson, *L'espace théâtrale médiéval* (Paris, 1975), 15–37. Konigson, with some qualifications, supports Heinz.

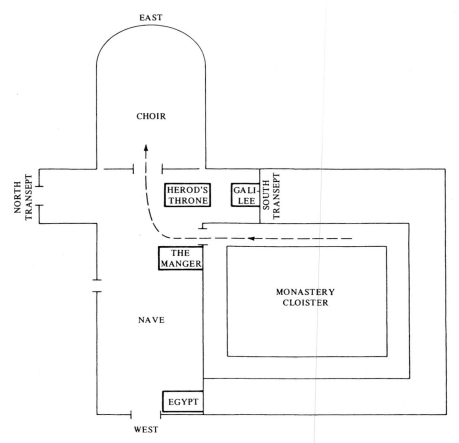

EAST

CHOIR

NORTH TRANSEPT

HEROD'S THRONE

GALI-LEE

SOUTH TRANSEPT

THE MANGER

MONASTERY CLOISTER

NAVE

EGYPT

WEST

1. Plan of the Church of St. Benoît-sur-Loire (Fleury) showing possible acting locations for the play *The Slaughter of the Innocents*. Dotted line shows the processional route for the children. Based on Arnold Williams, *The Drama of Medieval England* (Michigan State University Press, 1961), and reproduced from David Bevington, *Medieval Drama*, copyright © 1975 by Houghton Mifflin Company. Used by permission of the publishers.

cession des prophètes" places the fiery furnace of Nebuchadnezzar.[3] Spatial arrangements naturally varied somewhat from cathedral to cathedral, as specific shrines or chapels provided locations with particularly strong symbolic value for certain stories, but the basic strategies in the use of spatial and figurative connotation to reinforce the liturgical performances were found wherever these were offered (Fig. 1).

[3]Gustave Cohen, *Anthologie du drame liturgique en France au Moyen-Age* (Paris, 1955), 66, 120–40; Karl Young, *The Drama of the Medieval Church*, 2 vols. (Oxford, 1933), 2:75–80, 154–65.

Early-twentieth-century scholars considered the mystery plays presented outside the church to be direct descendants of these liturgical dramas, but more recent research has challenged this theory, citing as evidence not only the historical overlap of the forms, but their many important differences in organization, themes, and social function.[4] Nevertheless in the matters of spatial and urban signification, liturgical and mystery performances had important similarities. The general east-west symbolism predated the construction of the great cathedrals and was by no means restricted to them. A similar symbolic system was to be found in almost every outdoor organization of medieval drama where the physical configuration would allow it. At Frankfurt (ca. 1350), Lucerne (1583), and Donaueschingen (ca. 1600), to take only three famous examples, there was a platform representing Heaven to the east, like the high altar in a cathedral, an infernal Hell-Mouth at the opposite western end, and earthly locations scattered between. Frankfurt and Lucerne both used a temple as an element to define this central area, and all three placed the crucifixion midway between the earthly center and paradise (Fig. 2).

Cities offered a variety of richly significant locations for the performance of religious drama. In many of them the space immediately adjacent to the cathedral was apparently employed, as for the famous medieval play, the *Jeu d'Adam*, with the cathedral as a whole serving as the abode of God and probably of the angelic choir.[5] Like the cathedral crypt, cemeteries and burial grounds served as defining locales for passion and resurrection plays, for example, in Rouen and Vienna.[6] Often a particularly favored locale was the marketplace, which like the encompassing city could be seen as a symbol of the stage upon which Everyman played his earthly role. The connotations of the market space made it especially suitable for this function. Usually contiguous to the town hall, surrounded by the dwellings and places of business of the city's mercantile leaders, itself the center for trade, recreation, and social intercourse, it was in fact the stage on which the new urban bourgeois class played out their lives, the secular if not the geographical heart of the city, as the cathedral was the spiritual heart (though these two orientations were not as clearly separated as they later became, business organizations such as the medieval guilds still having an important religious component). The mystery plays, written in the vernacular and stressing the similarity between the physical world of

[4]Most notably O. B. Hardison, *Christian Rite and Christian Drama in the Middle Ages* (Baltimore, 1965).

[5]Grace Frank, "Genesis and Staging of the *Jeu d'Adam*," PMLA 39 (1944), 7–17.

[6]Gustave Cohen, *Histoire de la mise en scène dans le théâtre religieux français du Moyen-Âge* (Paris, 1951), 65.

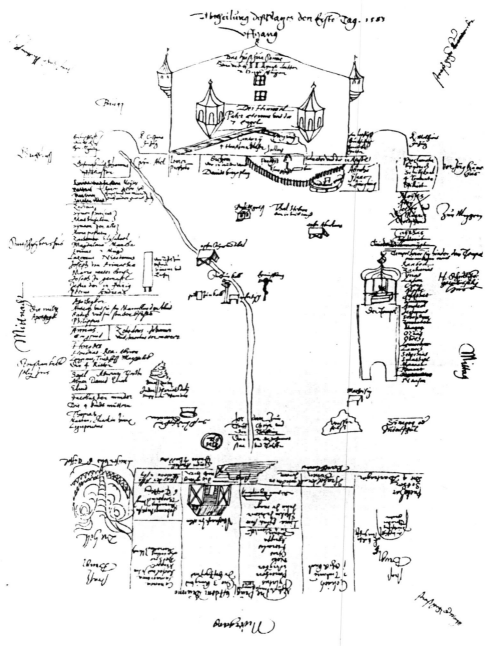

2. Stage plan for the first day of the 1583 passion play in the Lucerne Fischmarkt. Heaven is placed against the permanent building at the top, where the action begins. Other structures—the largest are the temple on the right side of the marketplace, and the Hell-Mouth (upsidedown in this drawing) at the lower left—for various later scenes are scattered about the open area. Characters are listed next to their stations. From Franz Leibing, *Die Inszenierung des zweitätigen luzernes Österspiels* (1869).

their biblical subjects and that of their audience, were extremely well served by a space redolent of those vernacular and contemporary concerns, just as the more abstract and ritualistic liturgical drama was well served by the surrounding iconography of the cathedral.

On a grander scale, the city as a whole could also be utilized as a theatrical space. Indeed Lewis Mumford sees that as one of its central functions: "Whatever the practical needs of the Medieval town, it was above all things, in its busy turbulent life, a stage for the ceremonies of the Church. Therein lay its drama and its ideal consummation." The key to the medieval city Mumford finds in the moving pageant or procession,

> above all in the great religious procession that winds about the streets and places before it finally debouches into the church or the cathedral for the great ceremony itself. These great processions united, as did the ceremonies of the church, spectators, communicants, and participants. Even the tortuous windings of the Medieval streets contributed to this effect, by affording those in the procession glimpses of other participants so that they became spectators as well, as they can never be in a formal parade on a straight street.[7]

These great processions and the dramatic pageants that, like them, moved through the medieval city, by claiming that entire city as their setting, also made a claim for the involvement of every citizen that went even beyond that of the great spectacles in the marketplace. But though the dramatic performances may not have directly involved the same large numbers of citizens as the great processions, they still encouraged active participation by regularly erasing any possible barrier between performance and public space. The Viennese passion of the fifteenth century that began in the marketplace doubtless assumed the secular and social connotations of that area, but when the actor portraying Christ subsequently bore his cross through the winding streets of the city to the distant cemetery where the crucifixion was to be represented, the spectators along his path were drawn even more directly into the symbolic world of the play, becoming active participants in the cosmic drama of sacrifice and redemption in a city that during this performance took on the connotations of the universal city, Jerusalem.[8]

[7]Lewis Mumford, *The City in History* (New York, 1961), 277, 291.
[8]Jean Jacquot, *La vie théâtrale au temps de la Renaissance*, quoted in Konigson, *L'espace*, 95. On pp. 77–110, Konigson discusses the relationship between medieval ideal views of the city and actual medieval theatrical spaces.

In the later Middle Ages the religious and dramatic processions shared the urban stage with another sort of procession, outwardly similar but with a radically different set of connotations, the royal entry. Many religious processions proceeded from one of the city gates to the cathedral, a trajectory symbolizing the approach to the spiritual center of the community, though other trajectories—even the totally opposite one from city center to edge—were possible, as the Viennese passion demonstrates. Such flexibility was impossible for the entry, which, representing the welcome to the city of an important guest, necessarily had to move from the gates (a major symbolic location for this sort of ceremony) to the center, represented usually by the cathedral or the palace that was to house the privileged visitor. The early royal entries were essentially little more than such welcomes, but as the sovereign power increased and the autonomy of the city declined, the connotations of these ceremonies reflected the change. The opening of the city gates or the presentation of the keys to them came to symbolize submission and acknowledgment of superior power, and the procession to the city's heart became an act of possession and a demonstration of authority.[9]

No longer was the princely visitor greeted along this pathway by symbols of the city's wealth, power, and prosperity; he was met instead by monuments and allegorical paintings and tableaux reflecting his own significance (Fig. 3). The city was still used as a theatre space, but one appropriated from its inhabitants by the prince. Once this usurpation was completed, the city was no longer available as stage primarily for the separate scenes of the citizens' dramas—marriage and funeral processions or civic-religious pageantry—but became rather the scene for the display of princely power, at which citizens were present by sufferance—as spectators only.

The physical arrangement of the medieval city was in many ways unsuitable for these displays of princely power. Whatever the allegorical symbols of dominance and authority gathered on the tableaux vivants that were placed along the prince's route, the message conveyed by the urban space itself was very different. The narrow and tortuous medieval streets, with overhanging structures and capricious widenings and narrowings, suggested no connotations of subservience or even tractability, but rather those of a stubborn individuality. The path

[9]See B. Guenée and F. Lehoux, Les entrées royales françaises de 1328 à 1515 (Paris, 1968), and Jean Jacquot, "La fête princière" in Histoire des spectacles, ed. Guy Dumur (Paris, 1965).

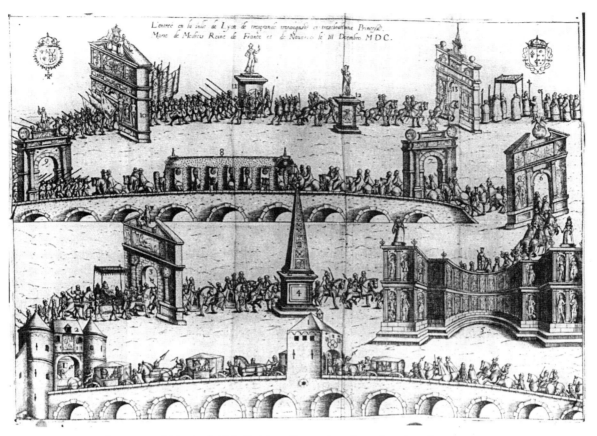

3. The entry of Marie de' Medici into Lyons in 1600, showing the monuments erected for royal entries at various locations in the city. Used by permission of the Warburg Institute.

the prince followed to the heart of the city was not an easy one, and it suggested in terms of spatial dynamics less a triumphant procession than the rather uneasy threading of a potentially menacing labyrinth.

For the new political power to display itself properly on the urban stage, new spatial structures were necessary, as they had been in classical times when the democratic Greek city gave way to the autocratic Hellenistic one. Here also the city ceased to be a stage where each citizen had a role with a contribution to make and became instead a showplace for centralized power. The great triumphs and coronations of the Hellenistic period could not have been physically accommodated in the narrow and winding streets of fifth-century Athens. Broad sweeping avenues were necessary to make the Hellenistic city suitable as "an arena for public shows: a container for spectators."[10]

Eventually, as the new rulers of the Renaissance consolidated their power, they began to impose their own demands upon the urban text, reforging it gradually into the baroque city, a more proper stage for the display of their magnificence. The royal entries may be considered the first step toward that restructured city, followed by the Renaissance spectacles and the development of aristocratic spaces in cities such as Renaissance Florence. The royal entries almost from the beginning encouraged a transformation of the urban text as they encountered it. For the entry of Charles VI into Paris in 1380 the streets and squares were so hung with tapestries that they resembled temples, and from many artificial fountains, milk, water, and wine flowed in abundance.[11] Such fountains and tapestries not only served decorative and allegorical purposes, but, as Konigson observed, also functioned "to superimpose on the actual city a idealized path, while removing the lived space."[12]

The idealization of the path followed by the royal entry in fact had much in common with the triumphal thoroughfare, an actual urban feature of the Hellenistic period. Closely allied to this spatial vision was the pictorial convention of perspective, which emphasized the order imposed upon space by the political master of that space, the centrality of that master's vision, and the increasing insignificance of objects as they were located at greater distance from the position of power. Michel Foucault cites a principle attributed to the Greeks, that arithmetic should be the concern of democratic cities "since it teaches relationships of equality," while geometry should be taught in oligarchies, "since it shows proportions in inequality."[13] Little wonder then that perspective became a central sign device for the new princes of the Renaissance in Italy. For the Medici, says Ludovico Zorzi, perspective became "the methodological vehicle for a political discourse, which imposed itself on the objects elaborated by medieval culture (the city being a representative example) in order to modify and adapt them to the ends of its own egocentric ordering of knowledge."[14]

This process can be seen literally at work in the Entry of Henri II into Lyons in 1548. In addition to the usual covering of the facades along the route of the procession, screens were set up at intersections mask-

[10]Mumford, *City*, 201.
[11]Guenée and Lehoux, *Entrées*, 56.
[12]Konigson, *L'espace*, 197.
[13]Michel Foucault, *L'ordre du discours* (Paris, 1971), 20.
[14]Ludovic Zorzi, *Il teatro e la città* (Turin, 1977), 64.

ing the tortuous streets of the medieval town with false perspectives painted in trompe d'oeil.[15] Iconographically, at least, the sovereign had already achieved the conquest of urban space which would be carried out in reality during the baroque period. The urban texture of the medieval city would resist this change for some time, however, and it continued to serve as a kind of ironic countersign to such ephemeral expedients as Henri's painted perspective or the temporary arches of triumph which were frequently built to serve as a more proper initiating sign for the entry than the more forbidding city gates, with their connotations of defense rather than subjection.

The idea of the baroque urban space was developed in the cities ruled by the Renaissance princes in Italy, and the theatre played a crucial role in the transition between medieval and baroque concepts of urban organization. Pierre Lavedan in his *Histoire d'urbanisme* thus describes the process: "Convergence and symmetry, these principles were applied to the city only after having been, one might say, vulgarized by two intermediaries: the theatre and the art of the garden. The theatre ties geometry to urbanism. Theatrical decor would have its effect on urban decor, while scenography was born from the treatises on perspective."[16]

Florence, one of the most active theatre centers of the period, provides a clear illustration of this dynamic at work. During the late Middle Ages Florence followed the typical pattern of employing its central open spaces for mystery performances, most notably a sixteen-hour cycle pageant performed in the Piazza Signori for the feast of S. Giovanni in 1454. Great civic and religious festivals and processions were still offered out of doors from time to time during the following century, but the revivals of Latin comedy, which began around 1500, were usually held inside, in learned academies and, more frequently, in aristocratic dwellings, particularly, as time passed, in those of the Medici. At the same time, Italian painters were exploring the spatial possibilities of perspective, a favored subject being the "ideal city." These interests converged in the theatrical designs of artists such as Baldassare Peruzzi and Sebastiano Serlio.

Before long, the vision of the abstract ideal city of these artists began to be applied to idealized depictions of the city of Florence itself. The scenic design created by Baldassare Lanci for the 1569 production of *Vedova* in the recently opened Salone dei Cinquecento of the Ducal

[15]G. Guigué, ed. *La magnificence de la superbe et triumphante entrée . . .* (Lyons, 1927).

[16]Pierre Lavedan, *Histoire d'urbanisme*, 2 vols. (Paris, 1959), 1:27.

4. Baldassare Lanci. Scenographic sketch.

Palace is a striking example of this development (Fig. 4). Brunelleschi's great dome for the Florence cathedral is here used to provide a terminal element for an imaginary street that the artist, in the Peruzzi-Serlian manner, extends directly back from the plane of his picture. Significantly, however, the central dome is not even mentioned in the contemporary chronicle of this performance, which notes: "The scene was the city of Florence, and represented a particular place in it, and this was the corner of the Antellesi with the facade of the Ducal Palace as seen from there."[17]

The Ducal Palace with its tower, now the architectural symbol of the power of the Medici, does indeed make a strong statement in this streetscape, even for a modern viewer, but for the original public, who were attending the performance in this very building, the effect must have been distinctly more striking. A setting of this kind surely worked to change that audience's perception of its urban setting. Leaving the palace with Lanci's idealized vision still in their minds, they would be encouraged to become more concious of the public spaces of the city as being appropriated, shaped, and defined by the new rulers.

Nor did this long remain only a stage phantasm, as Lavedan pointed out. In the direction opposite the cathedral, Giorgio Vasari was at this same time in the process of constructing for Cosimo de Medici the Uffizi Palace, linking the town center and the Ducal Palace with the Arno and providing a tangible urban example of the same use of perspective depicted in the ducal theatre. In the Uffizi were to be gathered under close Medici control all the city's major guilds and administrative and judicial officers, formerly scattered, in medieval fashion, in more independent enclaves all over the city. The design of the new palace employed the same sort of perspective as Lanci's stage design to reinforce this situation visually.

The marvelous engraving by Giuseppe Zocchi of the finished project shows the fulfillment in urban space of the ideas worked out in the perspective settings of the Medici theatres (Fig. 5). It resembles the Lanci stage design very closely in general arrangement, and the differences are indicative of the growing power and assurance of the Medici. The cathedral is retained as a visual reference, but it no longer in centrality or size makes so strong a statement, nor is it approached by a street vista. It is blocked off (as it always has been in reality) by intervening structures. The Ducal Palace, on the contrary, has moved toward the center of the composition and increased in size. The vista, more formal, regular, and powerful than Lanci's, now conducts the viewer to the palace and its public square. This is marked by a row of monuments completing this great urban axis and culminating, fittingly, with the equestrian statue of Cosimo, who created this example of urban scenography to express, for centuries to come, the power and importance of the Florentine Medici.

The theatrical appropriation of the cityscape by Renaissance princes

[17]Filippo Giunti, *Raccolto delle feste fatte in Fiorenze* (Florence, 1569).

5. Giuseppe Zocchi. The Ducal Palace from the loggia near the Arno.

was architecturally confirmed by the fact that this scenic appropriation occured, as in Florence, within their private architectural spaces.
When the first permanent theatre structures of postclassical times
were built, the great majority of them were located within the new
princely palaces. Some of the implications of this new arrangement
will be considered in the following chapter, but here let us continue to
trace the unhoused theatre, that theatre still excluded from any association with the post-Renaissance repertoire of architectural objects
but nevertheless a continuing part of Western urban culture.

From the Renaissance onward, city streets and market places continued to serve for the ancient forms of civic entertainment—the parades and processions, the mountebanks and medicine shows, the acrobats, farceurs, and mimes whose descendants may still be seen today in
the clowns, mimes, fire-eaters, and jugglers found in such popular ur-

ban gathering places as the square before the Beaubourg in Paris. The city around these entertainments has changed, but in general they have adapted to the changes without radical adjustment in the semiotics of their particular spaces. Processions and parades are still planned in reference to symbolically important paths and landmarks in the city text, and the acrobats and mimes, as traditional city market squares have disappeared, have sought out such modern equivalents as the pedestrian mall.

The institutionalized theatre of polite society, once having left the streets, generally abandoned them to this sort of popular entertainment, and this division remains generally alive today. Nevertheless, certain developments in the modern theatre have in some cases made nontheatrical spaces of particular interest for theatrical utilization once again. The modern organization of dramatic festivals in several European cities has been one such development. A combination of limited traditional theatre spaces and the desire of experimental directors to experiment with nonconventional venues has encouraged the use of squares, courtyards, and other urban spaces for festival performances, especially in southern Europe. In Dubrovnik, the discovery of new urban performance spaces has become part of the excitement of the festival, with the result that in recent years almost the entire city has been theatricalized. Nor need such activity be restricted to the period of a festival. Other Yugoslavian cities such as Split and Subotica have utilized urban spaces for performance as enthusiastically as Dubrovnik, if less extensively, to encourage civic pride, to stimulate urban renewal, and in general to reinforce a kind of utopian vision of the city.[18]

A somewhat different stimulus for certain theatrical performances to leave their traditional architectural cadre has arisen gradually from the romantic theorists' interest in local color and scenic verisimilitude. As part of his argument against the traditional unity of place, Victor Hugo insisted on the importance of site specificity in historical drama:

> Exact locality is one of the first elements of reality. The speaking or acting characters do not alone engrave the faithful impression of facts on the soul of the spectator. The place where such a catastrophe occurred becomes a terrible and inseparable witness of it, and the absence of this sort of silent character make the greatest scenes of history in the

[18]Dragan Klajic, "Theatre and the City," address presented at the Yugoslav Press and Cultural Center, New York, November 16, 1987.

drama incomplete. Would the poet dare to assassinate Rizzo elsewhere than in Mary Stuart's chamber? stab Henri IV elsewhere than in that rue de la Ferronnier, obstructed with drays and carriages? burn Joan of Arc elsewhere than in the Old Marketplace?[19]

For Hugo's contemporaries, and for the realists who followed, this prescription led generally to stage settings of impeccable authenticity, culminating in the realistic forests of Herbert Beerbohm-Tree and the authentic restaurant interiors of David Belasco. But another possible implication of Hugo's argument began to be explored only in the late nineteenth century, as experimental directors, beginning to challenge the proscenium stage, considered first other forms of staging within traditional theatre structures and then possible staging outside the theatre entirely. Thus, for example, the English Pastoral Players in 1884–85 staged scenes from *As You Like It* and Fletcher's *The Faithful Shepherdesse* in the woods at Coombe (Fig. 6), earning from the *Era* the enthusiastic comment: "Not only did the mounting leave nothing to the imagination, more even than imitating reality with photographic accuracy, it was reality itself."[20]

In a similar spirit the great early-twentieth-century director Max Reinhardt created in 1920 one of the most famous productions of the era, Hugo von Hofmannsthal's version of the medieval drama *Everyman* staged in the square before the great cathedral in Salzburg, using surrounding streets and church towers as auxiliary performance spaces (Fig. 7). During the 1930s Reinhardt also presented Shakespearian comedy, *A Midsummer Night's Dream*, in real woodlands and, in a particularly striking fulfillment of Hugo's speculations, staged *The Merchant of Venice* in a Venetian square, the Campo San Trovaso, which boasted a small bridge under which real gondolas passed and a picturesque house which, according to Reinhardt's research, had actually been the dwelling of a Jewish merchant in the sixteenth century (Fig. 8).

Since Reinhardt's era, this sort of theatrical utilization of settings that in large measure *are* the things they represent has been particularly developed in the cinema, which can control its localities far more effectively than can the theatre, but the Hugo concept continues to influence certain modes of contemporary performance. His idea of the room, the building, or the street as a "silent character" in great historical dramas underlies the enormously popular "son et lumière" productions developed in Europe in the 1960s and since spread around the

[19]Victor Hugo, "Préface à *Cromwell*," *Oeuvres complètes*, 18 vols. (Paris, 1967), 3:63.
[20]*Era*, June 6, 1885.

6. *The Faithful Shepherdesse*, Coombe Woods, 1885. From *Illustrated London News*.

world. In 1975, proposing a "sound and light performance" for the East Front of the U.S. Capitol, the president of the United States Capitol Historical Society described such spectacles as evocations of "history's major events on the actual sites where they took place, by playing— not on a stage—but on a structure and in the imagination of the viewer." The president reported that at that time there were over 150 such

reenactments

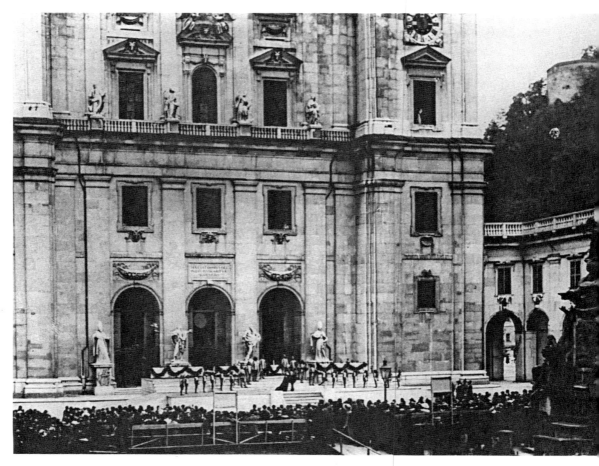

7. Hugo von Hofmannsthal's *Jedermann* as staged by Max Reinhardt at the Salzburg Festival. Courtesy of the Max Reinhardt Archive, State University of New York, Binghamton, New York.

performances already in operation, the most successful being at the Acropolis in Athens, the Tower of David in Jerusalem, Les Invalides in Paris, the Pyramids in Egypt, and Persepolis in Iran.[21] Something of the spirit of Reinhardt lives on too in such organizations as the Vermont Ensemble Theatre, an "environmental theatre" company organized in 1984, whose best-known production was their 1986 version of Thorn-

[21]Report of Fred Schwengel, "Sound and Light Performance on the East Front of the Capitol," Hearing before the Subcommittee on Public Buildings and Grounds of the Committee on Public Works and Transportation. House of Representatives, 94th Cong., 1st sess., H.J. Res. 621 and H.J. Res. 635, September 17, 1975, pp. 15, 17.

8. Max Reinhardt's production of *The Merchant of Venice*, Campo San Trovaso, Venice, 1934. Courtesy of the Max Reinhardt Archive, State University of New York, Binghamton, New York.

ton Wilder's *Our Town* with each act presented in a different church or hall around the village green of Wilderesque Middlebury, Vermont, and with staged outdoor vignettes of village life presented to the spectators as they strolled by lantern-light from one building to another.[22]

Another important inspiration for modern performances outside traditional theatre structures was found in the theories of Rousseau, who recognized a connection between the institution of theatre and the urban culture in which it developed, and, distrusting the latter, also distrusted the former. Both the institution of theatre and its architectural housing were banned from his ideal republic, which was to have only open-air festivals, civic celebrations.[23] Some subsequent writers,

[22]Leslie Bennetts, "Staging 'La Strada' in a Vermont Field Requires Invention," *New York Times*, July 21, 1987, C13, 1.
[23]Jean-Jacques Rousseau, *Oeuvres*, 21 vols. (Paris, 1821), 9:169.

such as Romain Rolland and certain socialist theorists, identified Rousseau's condemnation of contemporary urban society with a condemnation of capitalism, and his championing of open-air entertainments with an encouragement of proletarian pleasures. "A happy and free people," said Rolland, "needs festivals more than theatre houses."[24]

The conviction, stated by Wagner at mid-century and frequently repeated thereafter, that since the Renaissance the ruling classes had usurped the theatre from the populace inspired two sorts of reaction. There was on the one hand the movement that we shall discuss later, beginning with the Volksbühnen and still observable today in the new "people's" opera under construction in Paris, dedicated to creating separate but equal theatrical structures for the disenfranchised. On the other hand the followers of Rousseau frequently took the position that all such structures were in themselves embodiments of power and privilege and that the true people's theatre must eschew such institutionalization. Both reactions were operative during the period of the French Revolution, when the government undertook both to establish specific national structures as people's theatres and to organize great open-air festivals celebrating national themes (Fig. 9). The two traditions of Rousseau's interest in great civic festivals and Hugo's in the connotations of certain historical spaces merged in the great dramatic spectacles staged in Russia soon after the Revolution. The Proletcult organized modern allegories in public squares and recreations of episodes of the Revolution, involving thousands of participants, in the same locations where these events actually occurred. The most famous such production was Nikolai Evreinov's "Storming of the Winter Palace" in November 1920. The director proudly described his production as "a coherent action unrolling simultaneously on *three stages* of which two were conventional theatrical stages while the third was the *real place* where the historical event took place."[25]

The idea of a people's theatre without an architectural entity was widely accepted by politically engaged theatre practitioners in the 1960s and 1970s. In the small Tuscan village of Monticchiello, the town square once more became the site of annual theatrical performances, but now illustrating such populist concerns as political freedom, industrial pollution, or care for the elderly, in scripts created by the performers themselves out of their own experience.[26] The Yugosla-

[24]Romain Rolland, *Le théâtre du peuple* (Paris, 1913), 154.

[25]Nikolai Evreinov, *Histoire du théâtre russe*, trans. G. Welter (Paris, 1947), 429.

[26]Roberto Suro, "Defending the Environment Turns into a Drama," *New York Times*, July 21, 1987, A4, 3.

9. The Festival of the Federation, Paris, July 14, 1790. Armand Dayot, *La Révolution française*. Reproduced by courtesy of Librairie Ernest Flammarion.

vian political drama *The Liberation of Skopje* toured to dozens of cities in Europe and North America, always performing in exterior urban locations, preferably in two adjacent courtyards. Certain theatre practitioners of this period, especially in the United States and France, saw the street as a symbol of political freedom and the theatre building as a symbol of the "cultural industry," an "aspect of capitalism which must be destroyed,"[27] and thus created performances in city streets to draw upon these populist connotations.

In one striking contemporary case, this interest has led to an attempt to bring the street into the theatre structure—not to control it, as the Renaissance princes attempted, but to incorporate its populist connotations into the assumed elitist space. Florian Beigel of London's Half Moon Company looked back in the company's manifesto to the street origins of the theatre, before its "takover in the sixteenth cen-

[27]Jean-Jacques Lebel, "Notes on Political Street Theatre, Paris: 1968, 1969," *The Drama Review* 13 (Summer 1969), 110.

tury by polite society." In the company's new space, completed in 1986, the street in front of the theatre borders on a courtyard, and this in turn opens into a theatre space with facades designated as "notational houses," meaning that their window openings, echoing the real window openings in the adjacent courtyard and street, do not serve real living spaces, but may be used by either actors or audience members, depending on the production (Fig. 10). Notes one reviewer: "The street connection was bound to appeal to a lively company which prides itself on its community relations, its local patronage, and which sees itself as a radical and populist alternative to the West End."[28] This interesting attempt to blend the semiotics of the street and the established if experimental theatre space is unique, however. Generally speaking, the populist directors who have utilized the streets and other nontraditional urban locations during the past twenty years have not wished to repeat performances in a specific space, but have on the contrary sought new spaces for each production, spaces whose already existing semiotics would provide an important element of the performance. The city, as in medieval times, has itself been utilized as a stage, but now with distinctly more conscious political and social concerns. Richard Schechner, discussing the contemporary use of "found space" in 1968 hypothesized that the "American prototype" of theatre in nontheatrical structures was "the civil rights march and confrontation," which converted the streets into "public arenas, testing grounds, stages for morality plays."[29]

Like the organizers of the passion plays or the royal entries, street theatre directors of the 1960s and 1970s often utilized specific urban elements symbolically related to their performances. Thus the "Six Public Acts" performed by the Living Theatre in Ann Arbor, Michigan, in May 1975 were given in six city locations whose connotations were considered especially suitable for each play—a worship of the golden calf before a bank, a blood ritual at a military memorial, and so on.[30] Similarly Armand Gatti, for a production dealing with a figure from the period of the Spanish Civil War, rejected the theatre as a performance space on the grounds that his protagonist had "never set foot in a theatre"; to show him there "would have been taking him out of his element, cutting him off from his context, from the air he breathed,

[28]Peter Blundell, "Beyond the Black Box," *Architectural Review* 180 (July 1986), 48. This article contains a number of photographs and a plan of the Half Moon Theatre.
[29]Richard Schechner, "6 Axioms for an Environmental Theatre," *The Drama Review*, 12 (Spring 1968), 54–55.
[30]Brooks McNamara, Jerry Rojo, Richard Schechner, *Theatres, Spaces, Environments* (New York, 1975), 32.

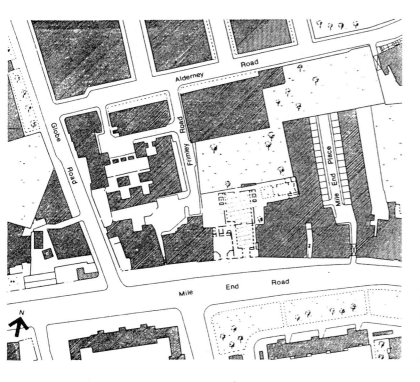

10. The Half-Moon Theatre, Mile End Road, London. The open courtyard and performance space is marked by small dotted squares, just above the word "End." Courtesy of *Architectural Review*.

from all that made him what he was." The most appropriate spaces for this martyr to the cause of liberty were the factory and the prison, and accordingly, the performance was created in an abandoned factory in Belgium. There Gatti made a striking discovery about the dynamic of creating this type of drama:

> with this kind of subject it's mostly the *place*, the architecture that does the writing. The theatre was located not in some kind of Utopian place, but in a historic place, a place with a history. There was grease, and there were acid marks, because it was a chemical factory; you could still see traces of work; there were still work-clothes around; there were still lunch-pails in the corner, etc. In other words, all these left-over traces of work had their own language. These rooms that had known the labor of human beings day after day had their own language, and you either used that language or you didn't say anything. . . . That's why I wrote in an article "a play authored by a factory."[31]

Such environmental experiments, as these examples suggest, are normally limited to a single production, though it is also possible that an environment may be utilized for a series of productions, which draw upon the same environmental semiotics and indeed develop new codes out of an accumulated performance experience. An example of such work may be seen in Vidlak's Family Cafe in Omaha, Nebraska, where a company organized by Douglas Paterson has for several years been presenting plays in a functioning diner. The diner interior is used iconically, with characters entering or leaving by the same doors as patrons and using the same space and material objects (Fig. 11). The plays are written specifically with this diner in mind, including even such features as its wall decorations, and certain recurring characters are now virtually accepted by the audiences as "regulars" of the diner.

Hugo suggested that the physical surroundings of historical events could be regarded as "silent characters" in those events. Gatti's statement, with even clearer semiotic implications, suggests that not just the great events of history, but the less spectacular stories of persons like his half-forgotten political martyr must be told in part in the "language" of their physical surroundings. His factory, like Paterson's diner, demonstrates that almost any identifiable space within the city may become a performance space. Through performance it will inev-

[31] Armand Gatti, "Armand Gatti on Time, Place, and the Theatrical Event," trans. Nancy Oakes, *Modern Drama*, 25 (March 1982), 71–72.

11. Laura Marr in Doug Marr's *Phil and the Gang Say Bon Voyage to the Carlyle Hotel,* a 1984 production in Vidlak's Family Cafe, Omaha, Nebraska. Photo by Doug Marr.

itably take on certain of the semiotic expectations of the theatre itself, but, at least equally important, it will bring to the theatrical experience its own spatial and cultural connotations, which the sensitive producer will seek to draw on to maximum effect in the work presented to a public.

2

The Jewel in the Casket

The theatre, like almost every public element in the Medieval
city, was absorbed and radically altered by the development
first in Italy and then elsewhere of the Renaissance and baroque court. The palace now replaced the cathedral as the center of the
city, and the prince became the focus of social orientation. The Italian
princes of the Renaissance, seeking to revive in their own domains the
departed glories of classical civilization, began the staging of classical
drama in theatrical spaces based on what were thought to be classical
architectural principals, derived from a study of the remains of classic
theatres and the guidelines of Vitruvius, whose *De Architectura* was
rediscovered in 1414. Even had their interpretation of these sources
been totally accurate, however, the altered social structure of Renaissance Italy placed theatre in a very different social context from that of
ancient times, and the physical configuration of the new theatres, not
surprisingly, reflected this.

The popular, public theatre of the marketplace continued, but was
accorded little official attention beyond what it had received in the late
medieval period—essentially the regulations of various sorts imposed
upon it by civic and religious authorities. The official theatre of the
new social order was that sponsored and supported by the leaders of
that order, the Renaissance princes, and these princes appropriated
both the art and its spaces for the support of their own social organization. Wagner somewhat hyperbolically but not inaccurately lamented
the results of this social alteration. The Renaissance princes, he observed, "took into their pay the arts whose lessons Greece had taught,"
and "*Free* Art now served as handmaid to these exalted masters," a
change reflected clearly in the physical space of the new theatre.

38

"Within the ample boundaries of the Grecian amphitheatre, the whole populace was wont to witness the performance; in our superior theatres, loll only the affluent classes."[1]

The first of the Italian ducal courts to become involved with the performance of classical drama was that of Ferrara, where Wagner's charge of the appropriation of the drama by the aristocracy can be traced in architectural terms with particular clarity. Medieval dramatic performances utilized the city of Ferrara according to the general pattern we have seen operating elsewhere. Pageants, processions, and entries began at one of the southern gates to the city, opening out to the river Po, then followed major streets to the central piazza, where were located the Duomo, the palazzi of the ducal family, and the homes of the leading merchants—the seat of both temporal and spiritual power as well as the central urban space open to all. Here were erected temporary scaffolds for the presentation of tournaments and the *sacri rappresentazioni*.[2]

The first classic revival in Ferrara was of Plautus' *Menaechmi* in 1486 in the Cortile Nuovo of the Ducal Palace, a location that strikingly symbolized the changing order. The cortile (courtyard) was called "nuovo" because it had been created only thirteen years before at the command of the duke, not from virgin land, but by the appropriation for ducal use of what had hitherto been a public square contiguous to both the palace and the main piazza (Fig. 12). Thus the traditional site for medieval performance was retained for the first Renaissance drama, but with very different connotations. Chroniclers of the period remark that the audience for these first cortile performances were almost as varied as those for the medieval religious spectacles, but they entered the cortile under quite different conditions. The piazza "belonged" to the general public, the cortile to the duke, who admitted the populace at his own choice. Despite the variety of social classes represented in these first audiences, this choice was already being to some extent exercised, since the cortile, a more limited space than the piazza, could not accommodate everyone who wished to come. A historian of the Ferrara theatre calls this limitation a "temporary compromise"—an accommodation of the principle of public access to the developing new idea of theatre as an art restricted to learned society. Within the cortile

[1]Richard Wagner, "Art and Revolution," *Prose Works*, trans. W. A. Gullis, 2 vols. (New York, 1966), 1:41, 47.

[2]Elena Povoledo, "La sala teatrale a Ferrara: Da Pelligrino Prisciani a Ludovico Ariosto," *Bollettino del centra internazionale di studii architettura Andrea Palladio* 16 (1974), 106.

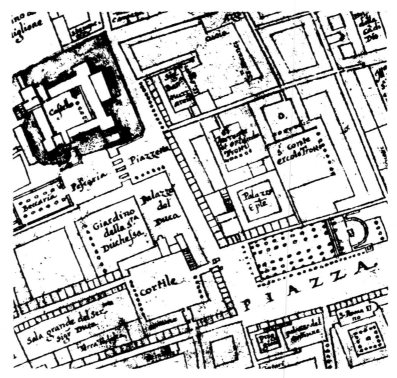

12. Location of the Ferrara Cortile. From G. B. Aleotti's *Pianta Topografica di Ferrara*. Courtesy Biblioteca Comunale Ariostea, Ferrara.

was the germ of a separation between theatre and general public that would grow steadily wider as the Renaissance progressed.[3]

Even as early as the second cortile performance, in 1487, the duchess and other aristocratic ladies did not enter the cortile at all, but remained in a more private space, the loggia to the west of the cortile, above and behind the more general audience space. This sort of spatial separation anticipated the later royal box, placed in an analogous position, and even more closely, the loggia at the rear of the auditorium for the ducal family in the oldest surviving indoor court theatre, built at Sabbionetta.

As other Italian cities followed the lead of Ferrara in the staging of classical drama, the cortile was frequently the site of such performances, and it is useful to remember that, as André Chastel has pointed out, the cortile was not in the late fifteenth century a long-estab-

[3]Ibid., 108–9.

lished architectural space pressed into a new theatrical usage, but a space appearing just at this time, as the palazzo itself was being developed as an architectural configuration. One of the developing functions of the new palazzo was that of the center of the social life of Renaissance aristocracy, and the interior open space of the cortile, a convenient site for festivals, banquets, and other entertainments, contributed in important ways to this function. The Medici Palace in Florence provided the major model for subsequent cortiles in Italy and elsewhere, itself drawing to some extent upon the model of the classical atrium, but even more directly on the medieval cloister, of which it was the secular equivalent, the "common place" of the palace.[4]

Thus as the princes appropriated the new theatrical art, the "common place" of their dwellings replaced the earlier piazza, the "common place" of the city as a whole. The Cortile Nuovo of Ferrara, not built as part of a palazzo but absorbed into the palazzo complex, was unusually large, but its function as center for ducal social occasions was identical to that established in the more conventional cortiles in Rome, Florence and elsewhere, and when Ercole I in Ferrara added revivals of classical dramas to these occasions, this practice was not surprisingly quickly taken up in cortiles in other cities.

After 1500 the cortile was gradually replaced by the ducal great hall as the favored location for dramatic performances. Once again in Ferrara the spaces thus used, first the Sala Grande of the Ducal Palace, later the great hall of the Palazzo Ragione adjoining the piazza, were essentially contiguous to earlier theatrical spaces, but if the geographical shift was slight, the symbolic shift was considerable. Performance space and audience space were now completely absorbed into the body of the palace and could be reached only by penetrating that space. The great halls, though some of them could accommodate a thousand spectators or more, were as a rule more limited and thus their audiences necessarily more selected than the open cortiles. They were moreover much less ambiguous as spaces. The cortile still bore many of the features of the public piazza, but the great hall was an unmistakable element in the prince's own spatial domain, the performance his possession, and the audience his guests.

In small cities such as Ferrara or Urbino, the great halls of the ducal palaces were practically the only interior spaces thus made available for these early Renaissance performances, but in large cities like Rome, which had more wealthy citizens or like Venice, which had a more

---

[4]André Chastel, "Cortile et théâtre," in *Le lieu théâtrale à la Renaissance*, ed. Jean Jacquot (Paris, 1964), 106.

scattered power structure, many aristocratic residences now began to equip their halls for such entertainment. In Rome Cardinal Colonna offered the *Mostellario* in his house as early as 1499, and in 1502 Lucrezia Borgia before her departure to marry the duke of Ferrara was entertained with a performance of the *Menaechmi* in the Vatican bed-chamber of her father, Pope Alexander VI, though a chronicler suggests that the space was little suited to such activity, there being "no scenery whatsoever as the room was so small."[5]

By the time that Palladio published his *Quattro libri dell'architettura* in 1570, the performance of drama had become accepted as one of the standard uses of the great hall, and the hall itself had replaced the cortile as the central public area of large aristocratic houses, as we may see from his description of such spaces in the *First Book*:

> Every well ordered House ought to have in the middle or chief part, some place with which all the other parts of the house may have an easy communication. Those places in the ground story are vulgarly called Entrees, Lobbies, or Passages, and above they are called Halls. They serve in a house as public places. . . . The halls serve for all sorts of ceremonial feasts, as weddings, banquets, comedies, and such other pastimes. For this reason, therefore, these places ought to be made much more spacious than others, to the end that many persons may commodiously be entertained therein, and easily see what is doing.[6]

In large palaces these halls could be spacious indeed, providing space for the gathering of hundreds, and occasionally of thousands of spectators, but as a general rule the public at large was rarely given access to such spaces, and admission was always at the sufferance of the palace owner, and not infrequently only at his personal invitation (Fig. 13). When Ariosto's *I Suppositi* was offered at the Vatican in 1514, Alfonso Paulucci, one of the guests, reported that the pope himself "stood at the door, and only those whom he selected for his blessing were allowed to enter."[7]

When the first permanent theatres of the Renaissance were built, they followed the architectural guidelines established by these earlier temporary locations. As early as 1518 Raphael designed a neo-antique theatre (never built) based strongly on Vitruvius for the cortile of the Villa Madonna in Rome, and in 1539 Serlio constructed perhaps the first permanent theatre of the Renaissance in the cortile of the Palazzo

[5]Gregorovius, *Lucrezia Borgia*, trans. R. Mariano (Florence, 1874), 414.
[6]Andrea Palladio, Book I, chap. 21.
[7]Silvio d'Amico, *Storia del teatro italiano*, 2 vols. (Milan, 1936), 2:88.

13. Performance in a great hall in 1581 before Henri III of France and his court. From a contemporary rendering, reproduced in Arthur Pougin, *Dictionnaire du théâtre* (1885).

Porto in Vicenza. During the 1560s Palladio erected in Vicenza both a cortile theatre and one in the great hall of the basilica. By the end of the century a few theatres designed as independent urban elements had appeared, many of them in structures located on the grounds of royal palaces or owned by the ruling families, but the major new theatres continued as a rule to be conceived as architectural elements within princely palaces. Thus the famous Teatro Medico created in the Uffizi in Florence by Bernardo Buontalenti in 1589 was located in a great central space on the upper floor of the palace, precisely that of the public hall described by Palladio, and Aleotti's Teatro Farnese in Parma was built in a room formerly for arms storage within the Palazzo della Pilotta. The fact that these performance spaces were enclosed within their owners' dwellings by no means limited their size or ostentation. The residential theatre designed by Bernini for Cardinal Barberini in 1637 seated three thousand people, and that built by the procurator Marco Contarini in his villa near Padua had a stage large enough to accommodate triumphal pageants and horse races.[8] As Italian ideas of theatre design and the Italian opera spread across Europe, the court theatre became a standard feature of royal palaces and a major element in the display of the glory of the European princes.

The development of such theatre spaces was not long restricted to princely palaces. Soon wealthy aristocrats and even well-to-do merchants were including completely equipped theatres, or at least halls readily converted to such purposes, in their homes as an indication of their wealth and cultural sophistication. Joseph Furttenbach's *Architectura civilis* of 1628 offered a theatre in the plans both for the "ducal palace" and for the much more modest "house for a private person." The ducal palace, Furttenbach claimed, was designed in the "Italian manner," and the architectural approach to the internal theatrical space certainly followed Italian custom, which developed not the spaces immediately contiguous to the palace entrance, but those well within, where guests could be impressed by such features as grand staircases and magnificent hallways before they reached the theatre itself (Fig. 14). Guests entering Furttenbach's model palace first came into an impressive entrance hall, past palace guards and their equipage, then into a large central cortile with a fountain, surrounded by columns, then into another large room, the loggia, which gave access to the theatre.[9] In the more modest private home (Fig. 15), the theatre was reached more directly, from the entry hall itself, but even though the

---

[8]S. Romanin, *Storia documentata di Venezia*, 10 vols. (Venice, 1858), 7:550.
[9]Joseph Furttenbach, *Architectura civilis* (Ulm, 1628), 21 and plate 8.

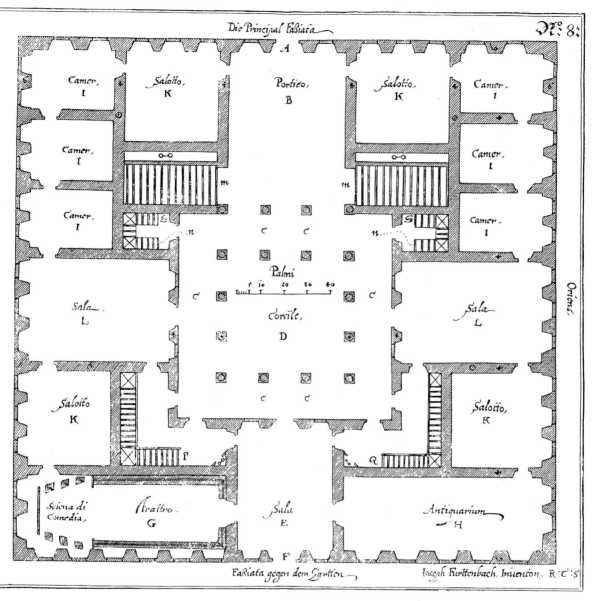

Die Principal Fassiata

Camer, I Salotto, K Portico, B Salotto, K Camer, I

Camer, I Camer, I

Camer, I m m Camer, I

Sala, L Palmi 5 10 20 30 40 Sala, L

Corrile, D

Saloto K P Saloto, K

Scena di Comedia, Teatro, G Sala, E Antiquarium, H

F

Fassiata gegen dem Garten Joseph Furttenbach, Inuention. R:C:5

14. Joseph Furttenbach's design for a ducal palace. *Architectura civilis* (1628).

The Jewel in the Casket   **45**

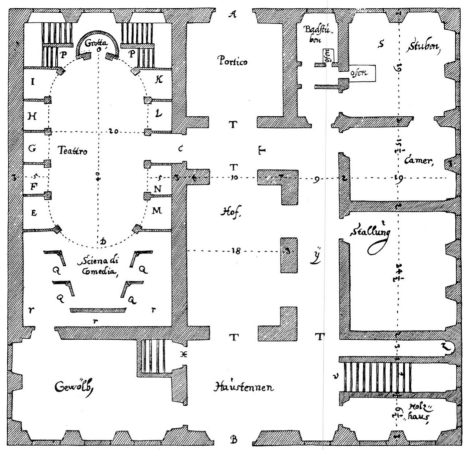

15. Furttenbach's design for a private home. *Architectura civilis* (1628).

theatre is placed in the corner of the building, with two external walls, no external access is provided. Clearly the theatre is meant to be regarded as a space within a private dwelling, with access only by way of that enclosing structure.[10] Probably an arrangement very similar to this was employed in Sweden's first public theatre, built by the German manager Kristian Thum in his private home in the south of Stockholm the same year as Furttenbach's treatise appeared.[11]

The first court theatre in the Italian style erected in France was also one of the most famous, a central feature of the elegant palace built by Cardinal Richelieu in Paris next to the royal Louvre. This theatre, like the building that enclosed it, was designed in location, interior arrangements, and decoration to reflect the glory of its owner in precisely the manner already established in the court theatres of Italy. The first sections of the palace were completed in 1635 and included a central living area set well back from the street with wings extending back further still to enclose a garden. A chapel was at the far end of one of these wings and a small theatre at the far end of the other. By 1641, however, a much larger theatre had been built, filling one of the two wings now extending from the central living block out to the street facing the Louvre (Fig. 16). As in the Furttenbach plans, this theatre had no street access, nor did it bear any external signs of its function. A visitor to it had first to enter the courtyard (passing through the customary arcade barrier), then enter the palace proper to attain an interior grand staircase that led at last to the theatre. The cardinal's will, in its disposition of his palace, reflected both his awareness of the symbolic importance of architecture and his continuing concern with the stability of the monarchy. The palace, second only to the Louvre in size and magnificence among Parisian dwellings, was left to be permanently the property of the king or of the heir apparent, and no one else, an architectural sign of their supremacy.

Between the building of the first Renaissance theatres in the courts of Italy and that of Richelieu, a quite different architectural and social model appeared in the first modern public theatres, strictly commercial ventures located, whenever local restrictions would permit, near the commercial centers of their urban areas. Though some of these (most notably the public opera houses of Venice) were owned by the aristocracy, their function was to make profits, not to contribute to the public image of their owner, so no architectural connection with that

---

[10]Ibid., 54 and plate 22.
[11]Nils Personne, *Svenska Teatern under Gustavianska Tidehvarfvet*, 2 vols. (Stockholm, 1913), 1:34.

16. Interior of the theatre in Richelieu's palace, 1641. This contemporary print does not show the raised dais in the center of the auditorium for the seating of the cardinal and his royal guests. From an engraving by Michel van Lochum.

owner was necessary. When a new Italian theatre was built in the later seventeenth century "all'uso di Venezia" (according to the Venetian custom), this meant primarily that it was planned for a paying rather than an invited public,[12] but it meant also that the theatre would be located in its own structure in a populous part of town rather than within an aristocratic palazzo.

In England, where elaborate court theatres of the continental type did not exist, there was nevertheless the same clear distinction socially, architecturally, and geographically between the public theatres and the converted great halls or similar spaces in Hampton Court, Richmond Palace, or Whitehall where performances were offered to the king or queen and their invited guests. The closing of the public playhouses during the Interregnum created a new role for those private performing spaces in aristocratic homes—as sanctuaries for the out-

[12]Nicola d'Arienzo, "Origini dell'opera comica," *Rivista musicale italiana* 2 (1895), 434 n. 2.

lawed drama and its players. A seventeenth-century historian reports that "in *Oliver's* time they used to Act privately, three or four Miles, or more, out of Town, now here, now there, sometimes in Noblemen's Houses, in particular Holland-house at Kensington."[13] The most famous of these aristocratic sanctuaries was surely Rutland House, where Sir William Davenant staged the first English "operas" in the first theatre in England to use spectacle scenery in the continental manner. The traditional connotations of the private theatre were still present here; the elaborate display of the Rutland House "operas" was clearly intended to impress Davenant's guests. But private performance under the political situation of the Interregnum took on other important connotations. In addition to representing wealth and power as lavish possessions of a patron, the performances, by being housed in that patron's own residence, were in some degree immune from the general legal system of the culture. The traditional English respect for private property, for an Englishman's home as his castle, seems already to have been operative here. In later periods, as we shall see, when state censorship created problems for theatrical presentation, private spaces within dwellings were often utilized instead because of these very different connotations.

The Restoration of the monarchy in 1660 removed any necessity for such an outlet in England, however, and subsequent private and court performances, never as popular as on the continent in any case, returned to their traditional role. The spectators were invited by patron or monarch as they might be invited to a formal banquet, and clearly saw themselves as guests in the patron's domain. When in 1675 an Italian *Scaramucchio* was permitted to charge admission for performances at Whitehall, the practice was so alien to the tradition of such a performance space as to cause much consternation. John Evelyn calls the innovation "very Scandalous, I never saw so before at Court Diversions," and Andrew Marvell noted that it had its effect both on audience composition and internal spatial arrangements: "all Sorts of People flocking thither, and paying their Mony as at a common Playhouse; nay even a twelve-penny Gallery is builded for the convenience of his Majesty's poorer Subjects."[14]

The idea for this commercial use of a court theatrical space probably came, as did several theatrical innovations of the English Restoration, from France. Since early in the century, the French monarch had al-

[13]James Wright, *Historia Histronica* (London, 1699), 23–24.
[14]John Evelyn, *Diary*, 6 vols. (Oxford, 1955), 5:75. Andrew Marvell, *The Poems and Letters*, ed. H. M. Margoliouth, 2 vols. (Oxford, 1927), July 24, 1675.

lowed a commedia dell'arte company to give public performances in a theatre in the Petit-Bourbon palace, shared after 1658 by Molière's troupe, in direct competition with the established commercial theatres of Paris, the Bourgogne and Marais. When that theatre was closed for a remodeling of the palace in 1660, Molière's troupe was allowed to move into the theatre built by Richelieu, now owned by the crown but never before opened to the general public. There they remained until 1673, when they were replaced by the newly formed national Opéra and the spoken theatre had to seek a more conventional home elsewhere.

England never established, as France did, a permanent public theatre in a royal residence, but occasional court performances continued to be open from time to time to outsiders. Colley Cibber remarks on the very different conditions operating at such performances, owing to their location within the king's own space:

> A Play presented at Court, or acted on a publick Stage, seem to their different Auditors a different Entertainment. Now hear my Reason for it. In the common Theatre the Guests are at home, where the politer Forms of Goodbreeding are not so nicely regarded: Every one there falls to, and likes or finds fault according to his natural Taste or Appetite. At Court, where the Prince gives the Treat, and honours the Table with his own Presence, the Audience is under the Restraint of a Circle, where Laughter or Applause rais'd higher than a Whisper would be star'd at.[15]

The eighteenth century was the golden age of the court and private theatres, the vast majority of them open only to highly select audiences by special invitation (Fig. 17). In France the liberation of manners, a taste for intimacy, and a refinement of culture after 1715 encouraged many in polite society to establish such theatres, and during this century France much more than Italy set the social fashion for the rest of Europe. The French court had its own theatres, as did various individuals there, but the real expansion of private theatres was among the aristocracy, and these reflected the social and cultural concerns of their owners as clearly as had the ducal theatres of Italy a century before. The usual emphasis of eighteenth-century private and court theatres was on intimacy, refinement, and elegance. Materials in them were costly, but carefully worked rather than lavishly displayed, and it was clear to audiences that they were a small and select company.

---

[15]Colley Cibber, *Apology for the Life*, 2 vols. (London, 1889), 2:214.

17. Private performance in an English home of *The Indian Emperor*. Painting by Hogarth, 1731–32, from a private collection.

By mid-century there were more than sixty such establishments in Paris and many more in the provinces. Probably the best known of this period, and a model for many others, was Madame de Pompadour's Petits Cabinets at Versailles, organized in 1747. Louis XV himself personally selected each spectator, and it was one of the outstanding favors at court, sometimes denied even princes of the blood, to be so chosen.[16] In 1752 a similar court theatre was opened at Fontainebleau, then others at the royal châteaux of Bellevue and Choisy. The most brilliant of these theatres was one of the last completed, that designed by Jacques-Ange Gabriel for the north wing of the Versailles château (Fig. 18). Members of the French aristocracy followed the royal example, commissioning leading architects to design private theatres for their residences, leading painters and sculptors to decorate them, and leading authors, musicians, and actors to provide their fare. Edouard-Charles-Franklin Brongniart and Claude-Nicolas Ledoux created theatres for aristocratic homes in Paris. Jean Philippe Rameau provided musical works for the theatre in the château of his friend Alexandre de La Pouplinière. Charles Collé regularly produced plays for the duc d'Orléans, who in addition to housing the national opera in Richelieu's former palace, now in his possession, opened between 1754 and 1755 no less than three private theatres in various houses he owned in the suburbs of Paris.[17]

Voltaire, the leading theatre figure of the era, encouraged the development of both monumental theatres as civic centers of culture and private theatres as locations of refined, intimate recreation. Throughout his long career he participated in private theatricals, in his own houses and in those of others. The theatre still exists at the château de Cirey where he and Mme de Châtelet began producing plays twice weekly in 1734 and where his *Mérope* was offered before its premiere at the Comédie.[18] Blocked by the authorities of Geneva from establishing a regular private theatre at his home there, he organized another at nearby Ferney, where appeared from time to time his protégé and friend Lekain, the leading actor of the period.[19]

French influence on cultural fashion in eighteenth-century Europe was sufficiently strong to guarantee that the fashion of private theatres in aristocratic residences would be widely copied. In Germany, the royal palace at Potsdam was clearly modeled in many respects upon Versailles, and it followed the French fashion of including in one wing an elegant theatre (Fig. 19). A court theatre was constructed in the Winter Palace in Leningrad in 1734, but the real flowering of private theatres in Russia occurred after 1750, when an imperial decree per-

[16]Adolphe Jullien, *Histoire du théâtre de Madame de Pompadour* (Paris, 1874), 7.
[17]Charles Collé, *Journal et mémoires*, 3 vols. (Paris, 1868), 1:398, 2:2 and 207.
[18]Pierre Pougnaud, "Les théâtres dans les châteaux et résidences privées," *Monuments historiques* 4 (1978), 21.
[19]See Lucien Perey and Gaston Maugras, *La vie intime de Voltaire aux Délices et à Ferney* (Paris, 1892).

18. The interior of the court theatre at Versailles designed by Gabriel. From Margarete Baur-Heinhold, *Theater des Barock* (1966). Courtesy Verlag Callwey.

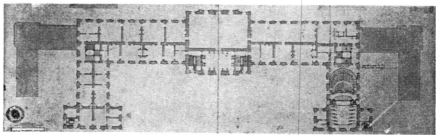

19. The location of the theatre within the Neues Palais in Potsdam, 1766. The theatre is at front of the right projecting wing in the frontal view. From a contemporary engraving.

mitted the performance of plays in private homes.[20] By the end of the century there were fifteen private theatres in Moscow and many more scattered through the provinces, especially in the Ukraine. Many of these were intimate gathering places in the contemporary French style, but the more famous ones tended to recall the earlier Italian princely seats for the display of wealth and power. Count Peter Sheremetov possessed three such theatres, one in Moscow and two on his nearby estates in Kouskovo and Ostankino, which surpassed in size and richess of display any theatrical spaces controlled by the state. In constructing such spaces within their private domains Russian princes sought, like their Italian predecessors, to display the theatre, like a jewel in a casket, as a personal possession, a sign of their magnificence.

The Russian princes were able to extend this ostentation even further, however, since their personal possessions included not only the physical theatre but the human beings presented as a commodity there. A French aristocrat could demonstrate his financial means by

[20]B. B. Varneke, *History of the Russian Theatre*, trans. Boris Brasol (New York, 1951), 69.

hiring a leading composer to create something for his private theatre or a leading operatic star to sing there, or he could demonstrate his political influence by obtaining from the court, as Voltaire did, permission for certain national actors from the Comédie or the Opéra to perform in his personal productions, but a Russian nobleman, thanks to the institution of serfdom, could actually purchase actors and composers for his theatre, just as he purchased rich hangings and crystal chandeliers to decorate it. The symbolic importance of this was not lost on French visitors, as we may see in the reactions of the French ambassador, the count de Segur, who was invited to a performance at Kouskovo: "What appeared to me almost inconceivable was that the poet, and the musical author of the opera, the architect who had built the house, the painter who had decorated it, the actors and actresses of the piece, and the male and female dancers in the ballets, as well as the musicians in the orchestra were all slaves of Count Sheremetoff."[21]

The Russian private theatres remained an important part of the cultural life of that country through the first quarter of the nineteenth century, after which they gradually gave way to municipal and state houses. In France, however, the Revolution essentially put an end to such ventures, as it did to the whole society of which they were a part. Indeed after 1789 the social image of the private theatre underwent a sharp change. In the public imagination of the new order, the mansions and châteaux of the aristocracy were often seen as domains of decadence and corruption, and the theatres within them, always symbolically highly charged, now took on new and darker connotations. Their clandestine nature and intimacy now in the minds of many took on erotic suggestion, and their elegance began to suggest voluptuousness. Historical studies of these "clandestine" or "libertine" or "gallant" theatres tended to place strong emphasis upon their presumed function of erotic titillation,[22] unquestionably a matter of great interest in certain of these theatres, but hardly a central preoccupation for the movement as a whole. Rather more extreme examples could be found in Russia, where the system of serf actors allowed for greater exploitation, but there too the notorious nude ballets offered by the Penza landowner V. I. Gladov must be balanced by the concerns of aristocrats such as Prince V. Shakhovsky, who provided separate quar-

[21]Louis-Philippe Segur, *Memoires and Recollections*, trans. anon., 3 vols. (London, 1825), 3:189–90. Several illustrations of the Sheremetov theatre may be found in Herbert Marshall, *The Pictorial History of the Russian Theatre* (New York, 1977), 15.

[22]See, for example Gaston Capon and R. Yve-Plessis, *Les théâtres clandestins* (Paris, 1907), and H. d'Almeras and Paul d'Estrée, *Les théâtres libertins au XIIIe siècle* (Paris, 1905).

ters for male and female actors and expected the strictest moral behavior from them.[23]

On the whole the fare at the private theatres of the eighteenth century was not markedly different from that of the state theatres which gradually replaced them, though they tended to favor the traditional aristocratic genres of opera and ballet, which provided a greater opportunity for spectacle and display. The erotic entertainment offered by some of these establishments is rather less significant as an indication of the taste of their sponsors than, as we have already seen in England during the Interregnum, of the relative freedom of expression available to theatres hidden away within private dwellings. On occasion this freedom allowed the performance in such theatres of material that might have aroused political rather than moral censorship in a more public venue. Perhaps the century's most famous example is Beaumarchais's *Mariage de Figaro*, banned by the royal censor because of its political content, but widely read in the salons of Paris, where it gained a public highly desirous of seeing it produced. A production was actually scheduled in June 1783 in the court theatre of the Menus-Plaisirs, but cancelled by the king at the last moment. Then, apparently at the insistance of the queen, permission was given for the premiere of the play in September at Gennevillers, in the private theatre of the count de Vaudreuil.[24]

Napoleon during the Empire installed court theatres at almost all his residences—first at Saint-Cloud, then at Malmaison, Fontainebleau, and the Tuileries, replacing the symbols of royalty with his own devices, but retaining the traditional spatial symbolism of such structures. The great period of private and court theatres was near its end, however. The aristocratic society that in the eighteenth century had considered the possession of such a theatre one of the signs of a certain political and social position was replaced by an aristocratic society that preferred public to private theatrical display. The boxes and the grand galleries of the great nineteenth-century opera houses became the new theatre spaces identified with this society. Aristocratic private theatres were still occasionally constructed, as at the castle of Chatsworth in England in 1833, at the château de Chimay in France during the Second Empire, and at Craig-Y-Nos Castle by Adelina Patti in 1891 (Fig. 20). More recent striking examples would be the theatre designed by Salvador Dali for the Parisian home of the baron de l'Epée, the "Sicilian" theatre in the Hôtel Boisgelin, with rococo woodwork taken from a

[23]Nikolai Evreinov, *Histoire du théâtre russe*, trans. G. Welter (Paris, 1947), 217–19.
[24]Frédéric Grendel, *Beaumarchais* (Paris, 1973), 404.

20. Adelina Patti's theatre at Craig-Y-Nos Castle, 1891. *Theatre Magazine* (1922).

palace in Palermo, and the elegant room inspired by the old Bayreuth Opera installed in 1957 in the left wing of the château de Groussay.[25] Such structures, though obviously the product of considerable wealth, no longer serve as socially codified signs of that wealth, but more likely reflect the whim or caprice of their patron.

A more culturally significant modern manifestation of the theatre embedded within a private residence recalls not the Renaissance theatres of political display, but the Interregnum theatres of political suppression. Some modern governments that have exercised fairly extensive censorship regarding theatre performance generally have been much less rigorous in monitoring work presented in private dwellings, even when this work continues for months or years and attains a rather substantial reputation. Normally it is not the case that the political power of the home's owner in itself guarantees this protection, as was often the possibility in earlier periods. Today it is rather more likely that the government chooses not to acknowledge such ventures of-

[25]Pougnaud, "Théâtres," 24. Boisgelin and others are pictured in this article.

ficially, sometimes because influential persons are interested, as they were in the days of Beaumarchais, in sampling forbidden fruit, sometimes because such theatre is seen as a harmless escape valve for the expression of dissident ideas, sometimes, as is apparently the case in Poland, because the government seems to be tacitly admitting that clandestine theatre is an important part of the national heritage. In Eastern Europe this form of theatre has been a significant element in modern theatre history. Early productions of the major Polish director Tadeusz Kantor such as *The Return of Odysseus* and *Balladina* were presented in such spaces in the 1940s. The Hungarian experimental company, Squat, forbidden public performance, performed in an apartment house theatre in Kassak, a suburb of Budapest, from 1972 until 1976. In Moscow during the same period, the Theatre on Chekov Street regularly offered performances in a room in a typical Moscovite communal apartment.[26]

Like traditional residence theatres, these spaces are hidden within buildings expressing another purpose, but the hiding is here done for protection instead of to demonstrate possession. Also as in traditional private theatres, the audiences are essentially guests, usually invited directly by the organizers of the performance or indirectly by word of mouth within a certain sociopolitical circle. Admission is normally not charged, though a collection may be taken. Although performances may be presented in the same internal space for years, that space will not be converted into a traditional theatre, in some cases because the experimental nature of certain works requires a totally flexible area, but also because such a conversion would make a claim for permanence and official codification as a theatrical space which might force governmental recognition and reaction. The internal decoration of such spaces thus has no connotations of the elegant decor of residential theatres of earlier times. Internal display here moves in the direction not of ostentation, but of camouflage. Ambiguous spaces such as lofts or storage rooms, or even spaces with clearly articulated alternative functions, such as family living rooms, are the preferred locations for such performance, since they can so easily be presented as nontheatrical spaces should the need arise. Both space and situation require an intimacy in these theatres considerably greater than in the so-called intimate theatres of the eighteenth century, and audiences of a dozen or so are not uncommon.

[26]The Squat Theatre performances in Budapest and the Chekov Street theatre are described on pp. 7–26 and 27–30 of a special issue of *The Drama Review* on private performance, 23 (December 1979).

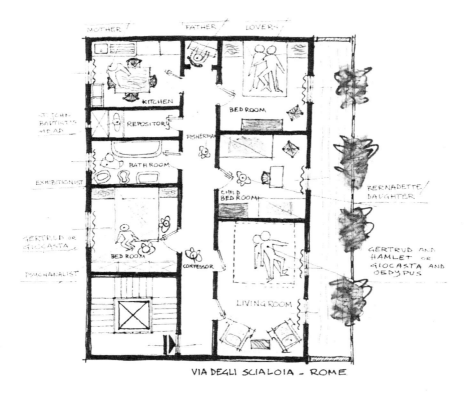

21. Plan of Silvio Benedetti's apartment in Rome, as utilized in 1979 for *Itiner-ario-Corpo*. Courtesy of *The Drama Review*.

Another contemporary variation of the theatre embedded in a private residence has arisen from the modern interest in exploiting non-traditional spaces for theatrical performance—probably reinforced, as we have already seen in our consideration of city spaces, by the interest of the romantic theorists, especially Hugo, in the connotative power of the actual space associated with a historic event. Thus we find performances within homes where specific rooms are utilized iconically (a living room scene takes place in a living room), symbolically (a bedroom or kitchen is used to take advantage of the symbolic associations of that place), or both. One example of the symbolically oriented use of such space was the *Itinerario-Corpo* of Silvio Benedetti, performed in 1979 in his apartment in Rome. Each of the seven rooms and the hall offered an enactment of a different psychopathological manifestation associated with that living space, which spectators could experience in any order they chose (Fig. 21). In a 1976 theatrical experiment by Jamie Leo, one spectator at a time was permitted to view a sequence of events enacted in a real living room and using iconically all the elements of that room, plus street noises from outside, the setting sun, and the subsequent automatic turning on of the street lamps. In this contemporary experiment we seem almost as far removed culturally from the original residence theatres of Renaissance Italy as it is possible to be; yet in one critical element of the theatre experience there is a striking parallel. Leo's spectator, like the Renaissance prince, provides the single eye for which the production is created. The elitism that has always been an element of private theatricals here returns in its purest form; theatre, generally considered an art form necessarily implying group reception, becomes at this point concentrated into its reception and interpretation by a single individual.

3

The Urban Hub

When opera was first developed in the late Renaissance, its creators generally fancied that they were reviving classical modes of performance, but in the event their experiments were so conditioned by the cultural assumptions and codes of their own period that the result was an entirely new genre. Nowhere is the difference between classical theatre and Renaissance opera more striking than in the physical spaces created for the performance of each. Hegel, in a section of his *Aesthetics* that deals with what we might today call architectural semiotics, contrasts the architectural symbolism of the Greek temple with that of the romantic church. The former is "gay, open and pleasing to the senses," a place "in direct communication with the world of external Nature," while the latter is wholly shut off from "external Nature and all the diverting occupations and interests of finite existence"—a place "for an assembly of persons to concentrate their numbers in one spot shut off from the rest of the world."[1]

The architectural symbolism Hegel found in ancient and modern religious structures applies in a number of important ways also to classical and Renaissance theatrical structures. The court theatres of the Renaissance and their architectural successors, the places of development of the Renaissance literary drama and opera, were, as we have seen, small, ornate, secluded halls, removed not only from external nature but from the view, indeed even from the consciousness of all but those selected few who were permitted to enter them.

Nothing could be more unlike such performance spaces than the

[1]G. W. F. Hegel, *Sämtliche Werke*, 22 vols. (Stuttgart, 1965–68) 13:334–36.

huge open public theatres of classical times. The Greek theatre, like the agora and gymnasium, was an essential unit in the urban model, an inevitable, accessible, and highly visible element in any Greek city worthy of the name. Pausanias, writing a series of contemporary descriptions of these cities, almost invariably devotes a significant part of his discussion to the local theatre, and the ruins of these cities still today bear witness that the theatre was a ubiquitous and dominant urban unit, often to the untrained eye the only clearly identifiable urban unit among the ruins.

The physical details of the classical Greek theatre have been the subject of scholarly debate for generations, but happily our present concern—the place of the Greek theatre within the Greek urban structure—is far less controversial. For our purpose, we need only recall that the Greek theatre, like its successors, was essentially a structure for the encounter of two spaces—that of the public and that of the actors. The heart of the acting area, practically and historically, was the orchestra, a flat piece of hard earth, contiguous to which was a *theatron*, a "place for seeing" for the spectators. In some early theatres wooden stands were built, but these were dangerous and unsuitable for the large crowds attending the theatre in a major city. Greek cities lacked the wealth, the labor force, and the architectural technology of arches and vaults which the later Roman cities utilized in constructing their theatres. Accordingly they sought sites that would provide natural areas for spectators, gentle hillside slopes, or, ideally, a hollow where a potential orchestra would be roughly enclosed on three sides.

Thus the Greek theatre, to a greater degree than any of its successors, was dependent on the natural contours of its site, and therefore was located in various parts of the city and its suburbs. Even so, some generalizations about siting are possible. A logical location was offered in many cities by the slope of the acropolis, the elevated stronghold that often served as the nucleus for an urban development that strikingly united architectural and natural features, as at Pergamon. In such impressive developments of natural sites, the theatre often played a key role, as it did here, becoming a "place for seeing" in a double sense. In many cities, including Corinth, Priene, and Ephesus, the spectator in the theatre sees before him not only the performance space, but a magnificent perspective of the lower city, the ramparts, and beyond them, the plain or the sea (Fig. 22). Such theatres serve a double function, like that propounded by Roland Barthes for the Eiffel Tower—they are cultural monuments in their own right and also mechanisms for presenting to their users a striking panorama of artificial and natural space.

22. The Greek theatre at Taormina rebuilt by the Romans. From Roberto Aloi, *Architetture per la spettacolo* (1958), courtesy of Ulrico Hoepli, Milan.

Occasionally a theatre is located near the base of the acropolis hill and serves as a kind of link between acropolis and agora, the traditional gathering place at the center of the lower town, itself thought by some historians to have been the location of some of the earliest theatre performances (Fig. 23). The size of the theatre normally made such an arrangement difficult, however, and more commonly the theatre is found in a topographically suitable area near the edge of the city's built-up area. Sometimes, as at Athens, the area selected is also one associated with the worship of Dionysus, the god most closely associated with the drama. Thus a combination of topography, convenience,

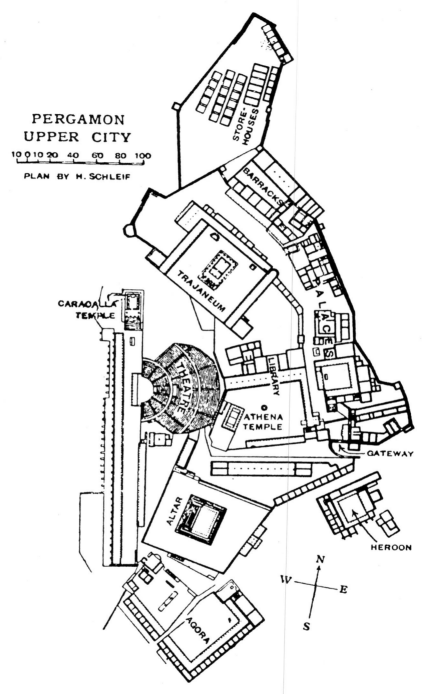

23. The Upper City at Pergamon. From Pauly-Wissowa, *Real-Encyclo-pedie der classischen Altertumswissenschaft* (1894).

and religious tradition determined the site of the Greek theatre, as it did the other major elements of the Greek city—the agora, the acropolis, the shrines, and the gymnasia. The city as a whole was a nexus of these elements, with residential buildings fitted into the spaces between these major units with little further specific planning.

A more regular geometric pattern of urban arrangement began to appear in Greece in the fifth century B.C. The first Greek town built in this new manner was Miletus, whose architect, Hippodamus, was named by Aristotle as the inventor of city planning. Hippodamus reportedly applied the principles of the Egyptian science of geometry to arranging a regular city plan, devided into specific zones, "one sacred, one public, the third private."[2] The theatre clearly gave Hippodamus particular difficulty; it stands out as the single rather disjointed element in the otherwise harmonious scheme of Miletus, located near other public spaces in the city center but not quite adjacent to them and set, because of the topography, at an angle to the rest of the geometric pattern (Fig. 24). Much more successful is the subsequent and similar plan of Priene, a city laid out on four terraces descending from the acropolis to the plain of the Maeander. On the highest was the temple of Demeter, on the next the temple of Athena, the theatre, and a gymnasium, forming a complex at the center of the urban space with dwelling blocks on either side. On the level below these, at the center of the town, were the agora and the temple of Zeus, and on the lowest level another gymnasium in the center, with a stadium to one side (Fig. 25).

Arrangements of this sort became more common in the Hellenistic period as developments in theatre architecture gradually freed the theatre from topographical considerations and allowed its situation to be determined primarily by its relationship to other elements in the urban scheme. The developed skene house and auditorium were linked together, and the advance, especially associated with the Romans, of supporting walls and vaults beneath the auditorium allowed the placement of a theatre on almost any terrain firm enough to support its weight. The exact considerations that determined the site of the Theatre of Pompey and subsequent permanent theatres in Rome have been warmly debated by archaeologists and historians,[3] but all agree that

[2]Aristotle, *Politics*, II:7, trans. Benjamin Jowett, in *Works*, 12 vols. (Oxford, 1921–26), 4:1267–68.

[3]See, for example, Giuseppe Marchetti-Longhi, "Religione e teatro, l'influenza religiosa nella construzione e nella topografia teatri nell'antica Roma," *Archiva espagnol de arqueologia* 26 (1953), 3–37; and Giuseppe Lugli, "L'origine dei teatri stabili in Roma antica secondo i recenti studi," *Dioniso* 9 (1942), 55–64.

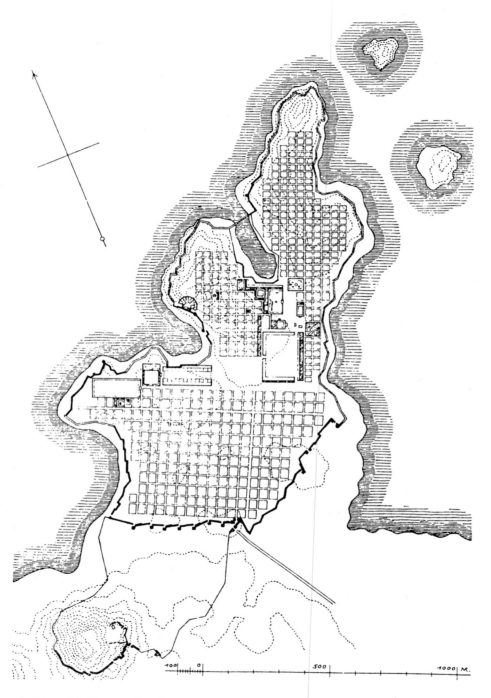

24. Plan of Miletus. The theatre is the semi-circular element near the water at left center. From Armin von Gerkan, *Griechische Städteanlagen* (1924).

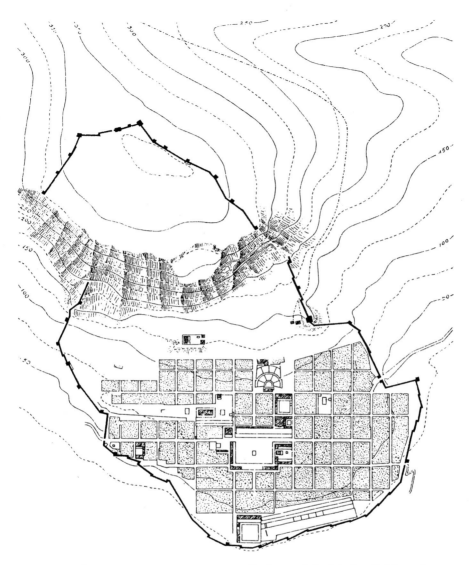

25. Plan of Priene. From Armin von Gerkan, *Griechische Städteanlagen* (1924).

topography was no longer one of these. Despite the availability in Rome of a large number of hillside locations perfectly suitable to a Greek approach, all these permanent theatres were built on level ground, close together in what might be called the first "theatre district," in the Campus Martius.

Cities of the Empire were often laid out in strict geometric form, frequently a square with major axes crossing at the center or to one side as at Timgad, Turin, or Aosta (Fig. 26). The theatre, as essential to Roman as to Greek cities, but more free topographically, was fitted into this chessboard plan with a square or two of its own, usually in a corner of the city or at the edge next to one of the major gates. In any case it remained, like its Greek and Hellenistic predecessors, a major and dominant element in the urban configuration, usually located at a major node of the city.

This cultural view of the theatre as a sort of public monument was, as we have seen, totally absent in the medieval and Renaissance concepts of theatrical space. It was not until the baroque period that something similar to the classical view appeared again in the placement of theatres within an urban design. The first postclassical public theatres were usually independent structures and visible, if modest elements in the urban scheme. But though in that way they were closer to the classical theatres than to the princely halls or the improvised playing spaces of the early Renaissance, these theatres clearly reflected an altered social role. The public theatres of Greece and Rome were major civic monuments, which held prominent positions in the urban text. By contrast, the first theatres of Paris and London were erected not properly speaking within this text at all, but clearly on its margins, in locations both precarious and ambiguous. There is no topographical justification for this marginality, as there was with the Greek theatre; it is clearly a physical reflection of the social ambiguity and marginality of theatre itself. For many years, especially in London, theatre locations reflected clear approach-avoidance tensions. Theatres were drawn to the lively heart of the city, but they were prevented from reaching it by the cities' public officials, the councils and prevosts, who resisted the establishment of the theatre as a legitimate part of the urban structure.

So long as theatre was performed in temporary locations by itinerant companies, the authorities in most municipalities proved generally tolerant, but tolerance ended abruptly when permanent buildings were proposed, implying a clear and continuing recognition for theatre within the social structure. Only the protection of a royal decree allowed a single theatre organization, the Confrérie de la Passion, to establish a modest home near the commercial center of Paris during the Renaissance. London's first permanent theatres, unable to gain the royal favor necessary to defy the antagonism of the city authorities, had little choice of location; they were built in the most readily available areas immediately outside the city jurisdiction, to attract a population for whom walking was still the standard means of transportation.

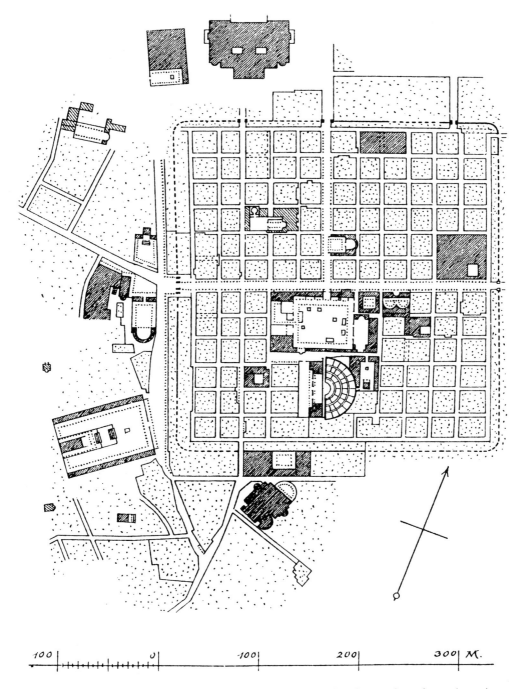

100 | 0 | -100 | 200 | 300 | M.

26. Plan of Timgad. From Armin von Gerkan, *Griechische Städteanlagen* (1924).

Thus was established a pattern that remained essentially unchanged throughout the period. The Renaissance public theatres in England were clearly socially "marginal," and this marginality was expressed consistently in their physical locations. Though widely scattered geographically, these structures were united in their boundary locations—inescapably tied to the city, but never truly a part of it (Fig. 27). As free-standing and distinctive structures, they were quite obvious urban elements, as may readily be seen in the various Renaissance engraved "views" of the city (Fig. 28); yet despite this distinctiveness they were not really landmarks in Kenneth Lynch's sense of the term since they were not, properly speaking, a part of the urban configuration. It was to be another three hundred years before London possessed distinctive theatre structures designed as actual urban landmarks. The few Renaissance public theatres established elsewhere in Europe were generally located, as in Paris, in more respectable sections of the city than those in London, but rarely did they contribute in any significant way to the patterning of their urban surroundings. Even in their best locations they tended to be tucked unobtrusively into small side streets, adding little of their own image to the district.

During the seventeenth and early eighteenth centuries, however, a new vision of the possible relationship between a city and its theatres developed on the continent, which gradually brought the public theatre from almost total obscurity to a prominence in the urban text rivaling that it had enjoyed in classical times. We have already seen how Renaissance theorists began to conceive of a new sort of cityscape, a rational structure devised to emphasize the power of the prince and often executed by his court architects. Under the papacy of Sixtus V (1585–90) a network of new streets, fountains, and churches was created in Rome, the first large-scale attempt to impose a coherent spatial framework upon the complex tangle of a medieval city. Projects of this kind naturally had an enormous appeal to the rationalist philosophers of the seventeenth and eighteenth centuries, to whom the narrow and winding passages of the medieval town were reflective of and perhaps even conducive to moral corruption and muddled, superstitious thought.

Such an attitude is clearly present in René Descartes's *Discours de la méthode* (1637), which in its early pages briefly considers the matters of architecture and city planning. Observing that buildings created by a single architect are as a rule more beautiful and better ordered than collaborative efforts, Descartes notes that cities almost inevitably suffer from a lack of focus for the same reason. "In the beginning only clusters of huts, they become through a succession of eras great cities,"

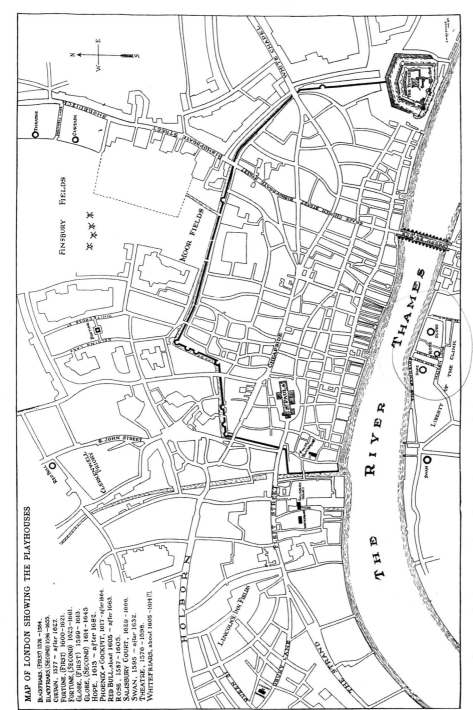

MAP OF LONDON SHOWING THE PLAYHOUSES

BLACKFRIARS, (FIRST) 1576 – 1584.
BLACKFRIARS, (SECOND) 1596 – 1655.
CURTAIN, 1577 – after 1627.
FORTUNE, (FIRST) 1600 – 1621.
FORTUNE, (SECOND) 1623 – 1661.
GLOBE, (FIRST) 1599 – 1613.
GLOBE, (SECOND) 1614 – 1645
HOPE, 1613 – after 1682.
PHOENIX or COCKPIT, 1617 – after 1664.
RED BULL, about 1605 – after 1663.
ROSE, 1587 – 1605.
SALISBURY COURT, 1629 – 1666.
SWAN, 1595 – after 1632.
THEATRE, 1576 – 1598.
WHITEFRIARS, about 1605 –1614 (?).

27. Map showing the location of London's theatres in Shakespeare's time. The dark line shows the walls of the city. Note that only the private theatre, Blackfriars, is located within them, to the west of St. Paul's. Public theatres are located on the south bank of the Thames (bottom of map), in Clerkenwell (upper left), and adjoining Finsbury Fields (upper right). From J. Q. Adams, *Shakespeare's Playhouses* (1917).

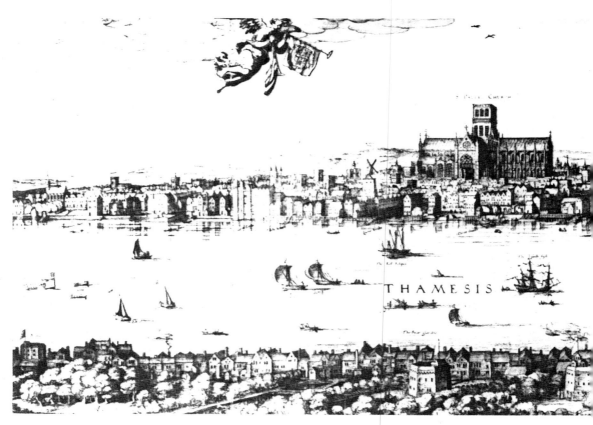

THAMESIS

28. Part of Visscher's panorama of London (1616). The three octagonal structures seen in the foreground, on the south bank of the Thames, are theatres. The Globe is the furthest to the right.

and thus bear little resemblance to the regular plan that a designer might trace in imagination on a plain. Individual buildings may be executed with art, but when we consider "how they are arranged—here a large one, there a small, and how they make the streets curved and uneven, we must admit that it is rather chance than the will of men using reason which has thus arranged them."[4]

This correlation between regularized city spaces and an orderly society proved extremely attractive to theorists and to those in power in seventeenth- and eighteenth-century Europe. As urban historian Josef Konvitz has observed, "Harmoniously constructed districts would call to mind the power of their author, standing out by the degree to which

[4]René Descartes, *Oeuvres*, 9 vols. (Paris, 1956–57), 6:11–12.

reason and reason alone determined their features." Such city plans provided "an example of good government in action that would induce and inspire good behavior in people."[5] New "rational" districts, even new cities, sometimes called "Cartesian cities," began to appear in France, laid out according to the principles of order, symmetry, and focus.

If public theatres, almost invisible in the seventeenth century, were to become significant elements in these new urban designs, the theatre itself had to be regarded in a new way. The rulers who had the power to effect urban changes had to begin considering the signifying possibilities of the theatre as a cultural monument rather than as a private possession, and had to begin looking to classical rather than Renaissance models for this new idea. This shift is very apparent in the first such theatrical monument built in modern times, the Berlin Opera House of Frederick the Great.

When Frederick came to the throne of Prussia in 1740 he undertook at once to elevate his minor kingdom to international prominence both politically and culturally. Central to these plans was a major rebuilding of his capital in the modern manner with great vistas, squares, and public buildings, including a new palace, an academy, and an opera house. As early as October 27, 1740, five months after his coronation, the Berlin *Vossischen Zeitung* reported that after considering building an opera within the palace (the traditional location), the new king had decided to clear ground in the center of the city for an independent opera structure (Fig. 29).[6]

In this, as in many other cultural matters, there is little doubt that Frederick was acting at least partly under the influence of Voltaire, whose campaign for the rehabilitation of theatre to its cultural prominence in classical times was a lifelong concern. Shortly before Frederick came to the throne, Voltaire wrote in a letter of March 30, 1740, that he would not consider the French "completely recovered from their ancient barbarism until the archbishop of Paris, the chancellor, and the president each possessed their own boxes at the opera."[7] Naturally Voltaire, who visited Berlin for the first time at the end of 1740, enthusiastically supported Frederick's building plans. He participated in the search for artists for the new theatre and in letters and essays called Frederick a Pericles who, by supporting arts and letters and

[5]Josef W. Konvitz, *The Urban Millennium* (Carbondale, Ill., 1985), 46.
[6]Louis Schneider, *Geschichte der Oper und des königlichen Opernhaus Berlin* (Berlin, 1852), 57.
[7]Voltaire, *Oeuvres complètes*, 52 vols. (Paris, 1877–85), 35:406.

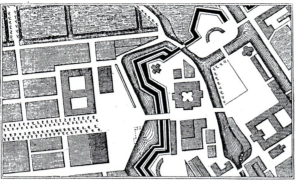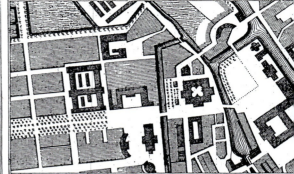

29. These two contemporary plans show how space was cleared for Frederick the Great's new opera house. On the left, the moats and castle ramparts are shown with the opera location indicated in dotted lines. On the right the opera stands in the middle of the newly created central square. From Louis Schneider, *Geschichte der Oper* (1852).

embellishing his capital with such magnificent public structures as the new opera, was making from the Lacedaemon of Berlin a new Athens.[8] Indeed no theatre structure since classical times could rival the grandeur of the building Frederick opened in 1745. The old castle ramparts and moat had been done away with to create a vast new square, in the center of which stood the opera, lavishly decorated on all four sides (Fig. 30).

In various essays written during the 1740s Voltaire called for Paris to follow the example of Berlin, to cast aside its image as a city of "Goths and Vandals" and to "bring light, health, space, and beauty" into the center of an urban area now "obscure, confined, hideous, and reflecting the period of the most shameful barbarism." In this embellishment of Paris, theatres were given his first attention: "We attend the theatres and are shocked to have to reach them in so inconvenient and disgusting a manner, to be accommodated in them in so uncomfortable a fashion, to see these buildings so poorly constructed, so badly laid out, and to leave them with even more suffering and embarrassment than was felt upon our arrival."[9] The preface to *Sémiramis* (1748) complained of the vast inferiority of French theatres to those of classical times and called for theatre buildings which would be "magnificent and splendid" public monuments, "facing only major public squares

[8]Voltaire, *Oeuvres*, 35:497. See also the "Mémoires," 1:23.
[9]Voltaire, "Des embellissements de Paris," *Oeuvres*, 23:297–98. See also the related dialogue, "Des embellissements de la ville de Cachemire," 23:473–78.

30. The 1745 Berlin opera, the first monumental theatre of modern times. Engraving by J. G. Jurck. Courtesy Märkisches Museum.

with peristyles and porticos suggesting temples and palaces." With such structures Paris might one day equal Rome, "our model in so many things."[10]

During the late eighteenth century a series of French architects and architectural theorists began to echo Voltaire's advice and Frederick's example and to champion this new concept of theatre as public monument, with the result that by the end of the century a series of such theatres had appeared in Paris and in major provincial capitals. The first was begun as early as 1754 in Lyons, where the architect Jacques Germain Soufflot designed a free-standing structure with austere classical external decoration for a rather restricted but central site formerly occupied by a garden behind the town hall. The opportunity to create this sort of theatre in Paris seemed to present itself in 1763 when the Paris Opéra, Richelieu's typical princely theatre within the

[10]Voltaire, *Oeuvres*, 4:499–500.

Palais Royal, burned down, with considerable damage to the surrounding palace. This event was quickly followed by a number of publications urging the building of a more public structure to replace it. Some theorists, among them the chevalier de Chaumont, emphasized the lesser danger of a major fire in an isolated structure,[11] but others, such as Charles Cochin, called for an isolated and elaborate structure primarily to embellish the city. Like Voltaire, Cochin wished to front the theatre on a major square, that facing the Louvre (Fig. 31), a location he called "the loveliest in the world."[12] This growing body of architectural theory was not yet sufficient to overcome the unwillingness of influential public figures to give up the theatre as a symbol of personal privilege, however. The duc d'Orléans prevailed upon the king to reject the various plans for a more public structure, and the new opera was constructed once again within his palace. Still, the setback by no means discouraged the theorists who wished to free the theatre from its urban obscurity and aristocratic bondage and to restore it to a position of prominence within the city. With the most obvious candidate, the Opéra, apparently unavailable for such development, attention turned to the Comédie, located since 1689 on a narrow, obscure street in a modest structure essentially undistinguishable from surrounding private dwellings.

The marquis de Marigny, director of buildings for Louis XV, had, like his sister Madame de Pompadour, a passion for theatre, and soon after his friend Soufflot created the Lyons theatre (which Marigny praised as "the only real theatre in France") he began to dream of a similar home for the Comédie. Soufflot actually began work on such a project but, when other tasks called him away, was replaced by two other promising young architects, Marie-Joseph Peyre and Charles de Wailly. Despite encouragement from Marigny, and through him, from the king, this major project ran into serious difficulties, some of which arose directly from the changing image of what a theatre structure was supposed to be and how it should fit into its society.

Traditionally royal entertainments in France had been under the jurisdiction of the Menus-Plaisirs, the responsibility of the Four Gentlemen of the King's Chamber, headed at this time by the duc de Richelieu, grandnephew of the great cardinal and patron of Voltaire. Although this responsibility included not only court entertainments but the administration of the official royal theatres such as the Opéra

[11]Chevalier de Chaumont, *Véritable construction extérieure d'un théâtre d'opéra* (Paris, 1767), 10.
[12]Charles Nicolas Cochin, *Projet d'une salle de spectacle pour un théâtre* (Paris, 1765), 33–36.

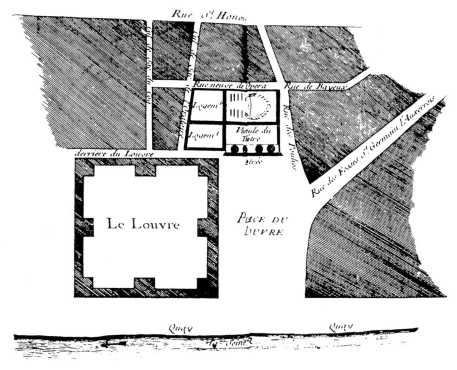

31. Cochin's proposal for the location of the New Paris Opéra, 1765.

and Comédie, the physical structures of these theatres were, as Voltaire never tired of remarking, given very little serious attention. When, however, the theatre began to be considered a significant architectural entity in its own right, not merely a found or flexible space but an individual building, a rival royal department, the Bâtiments du Roi (the Royal Buildings), began to dispute the sole authority of the Menus-Plaisirs in this area. When the new theatre at Versailles was built in the late 1760s, both departments were involved, but the Menus, after a bitter struggle, retained the upper hand, in part because the new theatre was still located within the royal residence.[13]

For the more public structure of the new Comédie, however, Marigny's Bâtiments was given primary authority, despite Richelieu's protests and political maneuvering. It was probably in part to circumvent Richelieu that de Wailly, who traveled to England, Germany, and Italy

[13]Alan-Charles Gruber, "L'Opéra de Versailles est-il l'oeuvre de Gabriel?", *Revue d'art* 13 (1971), 87–97.

to observe theatres in 1770 and 1771, made a point of stopping at Geneva to obtain the blessing of Richelieu's protégé, Voltaire. In a flattering letter of introduction, Pierre Hennin, the French representative at Geneva, informed Voltaire that it was in his work that de Wailly "discovered many of the new ideas he is pursuing, and he hopes that you will be so kind as to aid him in the completion of his plan with your observations."[14] This strategy, along with the continued royal support of Marigny, apparently convinced Richelieu that further opposition was useless, and he undertook instead to build an even more impressive public theatre in Bordeaux, of which he was provincial governor. Its architect was Victor Louis. Further theoretical support for such projects appeared in the meantime in the second volume of François Blondel's monumental *Cours d'architecture* (1771), which spoke glowingly of both the recently completed theatre at Versailles and the projected Comédie, observing that "nothing contributes so much to the magnificence of cities as public theatres, and these edifices should indicate by their grandeur and exterior disposition the importance of the cities in which they are situated."[15]

This should have left Peyre and de Wailly in clear possession of the field at Paris, but the retirement of Marigny in 1773 removed their critical support at court, and Marigny's successor, the abbé Joseph-Marie Terray, favored instead the chief architect of the Bâtiments de Paris, Moreau-Desproux, who had just successfully completed the rebuilding of the Opéra. The death of Louis XV the following year changed the power structure again, and the new director of Bâtiments, Charles-Claude de la Billarderie, comte d'Angiviller, and Finance Minister Anne-Robert Turgot joined forces to bring order to the many plans for the improvement of Paris and other major cities which, like the Comédie plans, had suffered from the confused political situation in the final years of Louis XV. Both Victor Louis in Bordeaux and Peyre and de Wailly in Paris were encouraged to move ahead as quickly as possible with their projects. The Comédie architects were invited to submit an article on theatre to the *Encyclopédie*. They described their current project in some detail, justifying it in terms highly reminiscent of Voltaire: "Our dramatic works have given France a superiority no longer disputed; but the stranger or the citizen who regards the monuments which embellish the capital will seek in vain for a *theatre* worthy of Corneille, Racine, Molière, Crébillon, Voltaire."[16]

[14]Voltaire, *Oeuvres*, 47:550.
[15]François Blondel, *Cours d'architecture*, 6 vols. (Paris, 1771), 2:263.
[16]Diderot, et al., *Encyclopédie*, 36 vols. (1778–82), 33:238.

In 1777 the well-known French builder, André-Jacob Roubo *fils* developed in detail, in a widely read treatise on theatre construction, the ideal physical appearance of the new style of civic theatre championed by these architects:

> It ought to be isolated on all sides and therefore situated in the middle of a square, the extent of which should correspond to that of the building it contains and to the space necessary for vehicles to circulate freely. This square should be entered by several streets, the main ones aligned with the main lines of the edifice, so as to establish suitable vistas, in order that those who are arriving can easily enjoy its aspect and those who are already inside can equally enjoy different perspectives which for that reason should be extended as far as possible. As for the monument, its form and decoration should announce its use; it must be elevated a bit above the level of the square and surrounded by porticos, both on the ground floor and upper floors, in which the audience can promenade under cover before and during the spectacle.[17]

All these features—the physical isolation, the multiple vistas that made these public monuments both landmarks and nodes in the new cities of late-eighteenth-century France, and the formidable exterior decoration, central to which was the massive portico—not only characterized the Bordeaux theatre (Fig. 32) and the new Comédie, but were echoed in a whole series of subsequent buildings in major French provincial cities such as Besançon and Nantes.[18]

By the end of the century the concept of the theatre as public monument was firmly established, at least in France, and designers elsewhere began to look to these theatres, and especially to Louis's Bordeaux project, as models. Particularly striking examples from the 1790s, though neither developed beyond proposals, were an opera house for Leicester Square in London designed by Sir John Soane (Fig. 33) and a new national theatre for Berlin by Friedrich Gilly. In fact the new national theatre, itself a model for many subsequent German theatres, was built in Berlin early in the next century by Karl Friedrich Schinkel (Fig. 34), and England received its first monumental public theatre in 1809 with Robert Smirke's rebuilding of Covent Garden (Fig. 35). Both had the usual monumental porticos based on the design of Greek temples. An 1833 description of London theatres, still some-

[17]Roubo *fils, Traité de la construction des théâtres et des machines théâtrales* (Paris, 1777), 24.

[18]See, for example, Pierre Lelièvre, *Nantes au XVIIIe siècle: Urbanisme et architecture* (Nantes, 1942).

32. The Grand Theatre, Bordeaux, completed 1780. Courtesy Weidenfeld and Nicolson Archives.

what suspicious of the new fashion, called the new Covent Garden "one of the most classical elevations in the metropolis, although of a character too solemn for a theatre."[19] Nevertheless an important part of the exterior decoration "announced its use" as Roubo had advised, since large statues representing comedy and tragedy stood in niches at either end of the facade, and on either side of the center portico were huge bas-reliefs representing ancient and modern theatre. At the center of the ancient group were Aeschylus, Aristophanes, and Menander framed on one side by the Muses, nymphs, and Pegasus and other the other side by Bacchus, Minerva, two furies pursuing Orestes, and Ap-

[19]Edward W. Brayley, *Historical and Descriptive Accounts of the Theatres of London* (London, 1833), 18.

33. Sir John Soane's project for a Leicester Square opera house. By courtesy of the Trustees of Sir John Soane's Museum.

ollo in his chariot. At the center of the modern group were Shakespeare and Milton, framed on the Shakespeare side by Ariel, Caliban, Ferdinand, Miranda, Prospero, Macbeth, Lady Macbeth, and Hecate in a chariot and on the Milton side by Urania, Samson Agonistes, the Brothers and Comos, attendant Bacchantes, and two devotees of Comus transformed into tigers.[20]

The new monied classes of the nineteenth century appropriated the opera as their central example of high art, and the monumental opera house became the architectural symbol of nineteenth-century high bourgeois culture. Consciousness of this symbolism is clearly expressed by César Daly, editor of the Parisian *Revue générale de l'architecture et des travaux publics* in a series of articles written in 1860 and 1861 on proposals for a new opera house in Paris. In each historical era, suggested Daly, the architect "has been the interpreter and the historian of humanity," because the dominant architectural elements of each society have revealed the focus and values of that society. Thus the Greek temple "best expressed the power of contemporary art and

[20]Ibid., 19.

34. Schinkel's Neue Schauspielhaus, Berlin. Otto Weddigen, *Geschichte der Theater Deutschlands* (1904).

knowledge," the Roman aqueducts, baths, theatres, circuses, and high-ways "expressed the force and power of the Empire and the Roman public," and the medieval cathedral and castle "represented the cross and the sword." Turning to his own era, Daly suggested that its great architectural symbols were the church, the opera, and the railway station, symbolizing renunciation (a virtue gradually disappearing), re-fined pleasure, and commerce. Every modern city prominently displayed these contemporary emblems, but certain cities might place particular attention on one of them, reflecting the emphasis of their culture. Thus Rome was associated more with religion, London with commerce, and Paris with fashion and pleasure. "In the entire world, Paris is the most elegant city and its population is as a whole the most polished and cultivated: in Paris the monument which best symbolizes this state of civilization and which most satisfies its needs is the op-

35. Smirke's Covent Garden Opera House, London, 1809. From Robert Wilkinson, *Londina Illustrata* (1825).

era." The opera "offers in architectural language the truest expression of the taste, mores, and genius of Paris."[21]

Thus by the second half of the nineteenth century the opera house had become an obligatory monument for any city anywhere in the world wishing to establish its European-oriented cultural credentials. Thus neo-baroque opera houses were built in Cairo, in the far East, even in so remote an outpost as Manaus, deep in the Amazonian jungles (Fig. 36). The continuing importance of this symbol in the twentieth century may be clearly seen in one of its most striking and controversial modern examples—the Opera House in Sydney, Australia (Fig. 37), characterized by its senior engineer as "a focal point and

Europe becomes classic to be copied

[21]César Daly, "Concours pour le grand Opéra de Paris," *Revue générale de l'architecture et des travaux publics* 19 (1861), 80–81.

36. The 1882 Opera House at Manaus, Brazil. Courtesy Transbrasil Airlines.

a civic symbol for a city which seeks to destroy once and for all the suggestion that it is a cultural backwater."[22]

As important as the splendor and size of the monumental opera was, of course, its location. An early project for the Paris Opéra, by François Bélanger, would have located it between the Louvre and the Tuileries, but the day for such topographical identification with the king or emperor was now past, and, as one architectural historian observed, the site selected was "no longer, as earlier, in a direct relationship with the court, but at the center of one of the representative quarters of the upper bourgeoisie."[23] Indeed the arrival of the Opéra did much to establish and solidify this district as a "centre de luxe"—a position it

[22]Michael Baume, *The Sydney Opera House Affair* (Sydney, 1967), 118–19.
[23]Monika Steinhauser, *Die Architektur der parisier Oper* (Munich, 1969), 157.

37. The 1967 Opera House in Sydney, Australia. Courtesy Australian Tourist Commission.

retains today. Roland Barthes's structuralist analysis of the "text" of Paris as seen from the Eiffel Tower identifies the Opéra district as the zone of "materiality, business, commerce."[24]

The location was further enhanced by the web of boulevards, many of them new, which converged upon the new theatre. The broad avenues connecting the great public monuments of Paris were Napoleon

[24]Roland Barthes, "The Eiffel Tower," in *A Barthes Reader*, ed. Susan Sontag (New York, 1982), 246.

III's and Baron Haussmann's fulfillment of both the baroque concept of urban design as an expression of imperial power and splendor and of the eighteenth-century visions of the logically constructed urban network. At mid-century Emperor Franz Josef in Austria undertook to rebuild the center of his capital according to modern ideas of urban organization, tearing down Vienna's medieval walls and replacing them with a magnificent new thoroughfare, the Ringstrasse. The first of the new monuments erected on this boulevard was a huge new opera house, located seemingly at the ideal spot to fix the center of the new city—where the busiest and most fashionable street of Vienna, the Kartnerstrasse, emerged into the new Ringstrasse. Despite its centrality, this location aroused considerable criticism, because the monument had no important vista leading to it.[25]

Haussmann would never have made such an error in urban design. Echoing Roubo *fils* in his call a century earlier for impressive vistas for the new monumental theatres, he observed in his memoirs that he had never laid out the path of any street, and particularly of a major artery in Paris such as those converging on the Opera, without considering the perspective it would open.[26] Michael Hays has pointed out how the Opéra boulevards link it to other "monuments" of the growth of French civilization: to the south, at the end of the Avenue de l'Opéra (then called the Avenue Napoléon III), the centers of royal power, the Palais Royal and Louvre; to the west the Place de l'Etoile and Arc de Triomphe, recalling Napoleon I and the Republic; to the north the railway stations (Daly's other major monument of the modern city); and to the east the stock exchange, the heart of the new commercial and trading society (Fig. 38).[27]

One might have expected unqualified admiration for civic monuments of this sort from Richard Wagner, who championed the great public theatres of Greece against the small, hidden, and highly selective princely theatres of the Renaissance, but in fact Wagner expressed a certain ambiguity about such projects. A Rousseauesque note of hostility to urban centers is struck in an 1852 letter to Liszt, in which Wagner expresses his desire that his operas be performed "in some beautiful retreat, far from the smoke and industrial odours of city civilizations."[28] Ten years later, in his preface to the first edition of the *Ring of the Nibelung*, he has begun to dream of a theatre of his own,

[25]Marcel Prawy, *Die wiener Oper* (Vienna, 1969), 24.
[26]Baron Haussmann, *Mémoires*, 3 vols. (Paris, 1893), 3:530.
[27]Michael Hays, "Lincoln Center and Some Other Cultural Paradigms," *Theater* 15 (Winter 1983), 27.
[28]Richard Wagner, *The Bayreuth Letters*, ed. and trans. Caroline Kerr (Boston, 1912), 6.

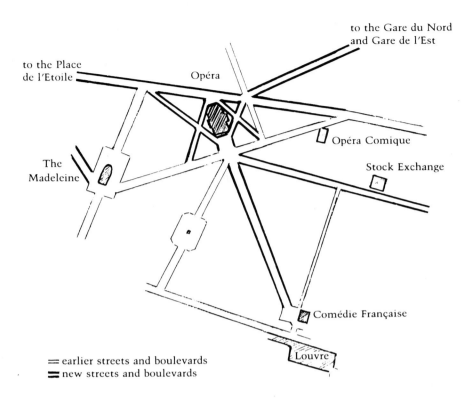

to the Gare du Nord
and Gare de l'Est

to the Place
de l'Etoile

Opéra

Opéra Comique

Stock Exchange

The
Madeleine

Comédie Française

Louvre

= earlier streets and boulevards
≡ new streets and boulevards

38. The Paris Opéra and its urban web.

but still not in a large city, where it would suffer competition from other attractions and draw a public whose primary interests might lie elsewhere. The best conditions could be found, he thought, in one of the smaller German cities, where his work could be presented without distractions in a temporary theatre, "as simple as possible, perhaps of wood."[29]

When the opportunity presented itself soon after, however, for a major monumental theatre to be erected for him in Munich, Wagner embraced the project with enthusiasm. Typically, the plans involved not only the theatre, but its entire urban area, as Wagner summarized the project in an 1865 letter to King Ludwig II, the sponsor. A major new street would be created, the Briennerstrasse, running past the

[29]Ibid., 7.

palace, through the royal gardens, straight on to the Isar river. A bridge would be erected over this to the higher bank, on the elevated terraces of which "the ideal festival theatre will proudly rise," as the culminating vista of the new boulevard.[30]

When this grandiose scheme ran into political difficulties in Munich and had to be abandoned, Wagner returned to his earlier concept of a festival theatre neither within nor on the periphery of a major urban center, but in a modest community where it would be the dominant spatial element. At Bayreuth his Festspielhaus marked one of the supreme expressions of the monumental theatre tradition. Here was no modest wooden structure but a huge edifice overlooking a small community which then as now it dominated both physically and symbolically (Fig. 39). Instead of a major urban landmark or the organizing node of an urban district, at Bayreuth the theatre became the central element of an entire community, a pattern repeated in subsequent festival theatres elsewhere, most notably perhaps in the old festival theatre at Stratford, England.

In many respects the opera house, as Daly suggested, replaced the cathedral during the nineteenth century as the central spiritual icon of European culture. The true predecessors of the Bayreuth Festspielhaus were thus not, as Wagner suggested, the theatres of Greece, but the great pilgrimage churches of the Middle Ages, supported not by a local population but by a public that considered the spiritual rewards gained there worth the labor and expense of a lengthy journey. Bayreuth might thus be called the Saint Iago de Compostela of late-nineteenth-century Europe.

The monumental theatre and especially the opera house still as a rule fulfill the symbolic functions associated with them in the nineteenth century—they serve, along with the closely related structures of symphonic hall and public art museum, as highly visible signs of civic dedication to the arts, especially the arts as defined by the high bourgeois culture of the nineteenth century (the basic contents of these structures, whether works of plastic art or musical or dramatic repertoires, also reflect this orientation). Such theatres, except for the special cases represented by the tradition of Bayreuth-style festival houses, continue to be located in major squares or urban parks near the centers of large cities, but outside the main commercial areas and often near luxury urban housing or specialized shopping areas suitable for so elegant a neighbor. In Germany the public theatre and in Italy the

[30]Wagner, *König Ludwig II und Richard Wagner: Briefwechsel*, ed. Otto Strobel, 5 vols. (Karlsruhe, 1936), 1:176.

39. The 1876 Wagnerian Festival Theatre in Bayreuth. A contemporary engraving.

public opera house have become prominent features even in towns of modest size, as widespread and distinctive an urban element as they were in classical Greece and Rome. The rebuilding of many German cities after World War II accentuated this phenomenon and more recently, as the governments of France and England have sought to "decentralize" their theatre and as many cities and universities in the United States have constructed their own theatres, the monumental theatre has served as the primary model for such development.

Although in fact many such structures have attracted a fairly democratic public, the traditional association of the elegant opera house with the monied classes led many nineteenth-century theorists, among them Wagner in his youth, to dream of a truly populist theatre, akin to what they assumed the classical theatres had been. The rise of the socialist movement toward the end of the century gave new impetus to this vision, especially in Germany, where the Volksbühne (people's stage) movement created Europe's first monumental theatres for the proletariat. From 1890 until 1914 the leading Volksbühne society, in Berlin, rented existing theatres for its productions, but by 1914 the organization was both physically and symbolically in need of its own facilities. In Berlin, as in Paris and London, the nobility and wealthy bourgeoisie gravitated steadily to the western part of the city, leaving the east for the poor and the working classes. In each of these cities the center and the west became the favored areas for major theatres (London's major entertainment district is still, somewhat anachronistically, called the "West End"), while only such modest ventures as the London "gaffs" or small ethnic theatres could be found in the east.

The new Volksbühne theatre significantly countered this trend. It was the only major Berlin theatre located in the east of the city, in the midst of the Prenzlauer Berg, a residential area for industrial workers. The motto of the society was incised in large letters on the front of this impressive structure, "Die Kunst dem Volke" (Art to the People), but its location spoke as clearly as its slogan (Fig. 40). Destroyed during the war, the theatre was rebuilt at the same site, which meant it was now located near the political and economic center of what had become East Berlin. West Berliners built their own Volksbühne in a park near the Kurfürstendamm, the leisure and entertainment center of the western city. As well as reflecting in miniature the division of Berlin itself, the two postwar Volksbühnen accurately mirror in their locations their own changed status; neither is now situated in a workers' area or caters any longer to a largely proletarian audience.[31]

Similar geographic tensions have arisen with regard to the Berlin Schaubühne directed by Peter Stein, probably the best-known German theatre of recent times. Stein's best known work was created at a theatre on the Halleschen Ufer, a hall set among working class tenements next to the U-Bahn in a rather rundown section of West Berlin far from the main entertainment district. With his artistic success, Stein won increasing support from the government and in the early 1980s moved into a monumental new theatre on the Kurfürstendamm in the heart of the city amongst night clubs and *cordon bleu* restaurants, where the streets accommodate more tourists than workers. Even before the move took place, Stein was concerned by its semiotic implications, "getting us branded as a theatre that has been fossilized, absorbed into the establishment, and has sold out to bribes (and I am not saying that there might not be a grain of truth in this)."[32]

The socialist government of François Mitterrand has undertaken a

[31]Klaus van der Berg, "The Relationship of Urban Space and Theatre in Berlin in the Twentieth Century," unpublished paper, Indiana University, 1985, 13–14, 23–24.
[32]Michael Patterson, *Peter Stein* (Cambridge, 1981), 156.

40. The Berlin Volksbühne. *Theatre Arts* (1921).

far more radical experiment in theatrical geography in its plans for the creation of a monumental "people's opera" for the working classes in Paris. The location of this new structure is as significant as that of Garnier's Opéra a century ago. Like the original Volksbühne, it has been situated almost defiantly well to the east of the established Parisian entertainment world, and on a site with the strongest populist associations, the Place de la Bastille. The square itself recalls the storming of that symbol of arbitrary royal power which began the French Revolution, and a column at its center commemorates the insurgents who died on the barricades in 1830. The square has become the traditional rallying point for May Day celebrations and other socialist demonstrations and was the location of a huge victory celebration for the election of the socialist government in May 1981. It is, moreover, an area surrounded by working-class residences.

All these symbolic advantages have outweighed the major physical problem that the available space on the square, the site of a former railway station, does not really provide the sort of area proper for a monumental structure of this type. As *Architectural Review* noted in an article devoted to this tension: "In the French Classical tradition, operas tend to be freestanding objects, encompassed by a colonnade and blocking a noble vista."[33] So established is this image of the opera as civic monument that it imposes itself even in this highly unsuitable location. The problem is augmented by the required size of the structure, because the opera, when completed (for the bicentennial of the Revolution in 1989) is to provide a million seats a year. If the dreams of its planners are realized, this new monument should become the architectural symbol of Mitterrand's socialist era as the Garnier Opéra was of the Second Empire.

A common development of the theatre as public monument in the twentieth century has been into the arts complex, where structures for theatre, dance, opera, and perhaps other arts as well are clustered together to form a kind of supermonument, an entire artistic enclave within the city. Probably the most famous such complexes are the South Bank in London and Lincoln Center in New York. Both were created, like the monumental theatres of the previous century, to demonstrate in a highly visible fashion the public dedication to the arts now expected of a world-class city, but other more commercial and social concerns have strongly affected the situation of these complexes within their urban surroundings.

The association in the public mind developed in the eighteenth and nineteenth centuries between the monumental public theatre and elegant urban districts has allowed modern urban developers to employ such monuments as foundations for the upgrading of surrounding areas. New York's Lincoln Center provides a particularly clear example of this practice (Fig. 41). The traditional historical northward movement of New York's theatrical district suggested that the next hub of such activity after Times Square might be in the Columbus Circle and Lincoln Square area, but far more central to the planners' concerns was the possibility of using the new arts complex as a keystone for upward social development of the tenement area surrounding Lincoln Square. According to the official handbook published by the Center in 1964, one of the main stimuli for the project was that in the mid-1950s this "vast slum area at Lincoln Square, north of the newly built Coliseum at Columbus Circle, was marked for urban renewal."[34] As is often the case, one person's slum is another's low-income housing, and an article in the *New York Times* in March 1960 quoted a Welfare Depart-

[33]Jean-Claude Garcias, "People's Opera," *Architectural Review* 174 (Dec. 1983), 12.
[34]*Lincoln Center for the Performing Arts* (New York, 1964), 21.

41. Lincoln Center and its surrounding neighborhood. The Vivian Beaumont Theatre stands to the right of the Metropolitan Opera, its facade largely obscured by Avery Fisher Hall. Courtesy Lincoln Center for the Performing Arts/Photo by Susanne Faulkner Stevens.

ment worker who complained that "powerful real estate interests" were behind the selection of this site, and predicted that "the entire West Side of Manhattan, from Fifty-Ninth Street to 110th Street is being redeveloped, and, except for two token low-income projects, will result in the removal from this area of the low-income groups, mostly Puerto-Ricans, who formerly lived there."[35]

Indeed by the fall of 1962 the accuracy of this prediction was already clear. In a major article bearing the headline "Lincoln Center Sparks Vast Renewal on the West Side" the *New York Times* observed that "Lincoln Square is, in fact, the middle section of a broad sweep of improvement efforts that are transforming the west midtown area. Lincoln Square serves as a link between the concentration of new

[35]*New York Times*, March 20, 1960, 64.

office and apartment buildings along the Avenue of the Americas below Central Park and the extensive redevelopment work going on west of the park as far north as Columbia University."[36]

The subsequent twenty-five years have seen the continual solidification of these trends. "Gentrification," with Lincoln Center as its base, has spread steadily northward, until this formerly low-income, largely Puerto-Rican area has now become one of Manhattan's most fashionable and expensive residential districts, beginning to rival even the long-established upper East Side in social status. Lincoln Center has not, as its early publicity promised, given New York a position of world cultural predominance, and its spoken theatre, the Vivian Beaumont, has never even achieved a stable existence, but as a cultural and social symbol stimulating the urban development of the surrounding area, this has been one of the most successful projects in history.

The South Bank Complex in London has similarly served to stamp a new image on an entire district (Fig. 42), although instead of the blocks of luxury apartments (included in its neighborhood in some early plans) which might have encouraged a residential development like that sparked by Lincoln Center, major office buildings have sprung up in the area, and the effect on the residential use of the South Bank has been negligible or even negative. Bernard Shaw stoutly and consistently opposed the placing of a national theatre on the South Bank, arguing that the tawdry neighborhood would tarnish the establishment's image, but the South Bank developers recognized that Shaw's view of the theatre's role in the urban text was long outdated, and that, far from taking its stamp from a questionable neighborhood, a major civic monument could now serve as leverage for upgrading its surroundings. National Theatre historian John Elsom has called the South Bank project "London's Brasilia, a conscious attempt to alter London's pattern of social life by altering its geography."[37] Except arguably around Westminster, the Thames had been essentially lost to social London, abandoned to warehouses and often decaying commercial structures. The South Bank was a bold scheme to reclaim some of the river, even at the cost of ignoring the blighted areas further to the south, on which the present complex resolutely turns its back. The result has indeed been the expansion of social London across the river into this part of the city, but without major effect on most of the contiguous South Bank land.

[36]*New York Times*, September 16, 1962, 81.
[37]John Elsom and Nicholas Tomalin, *The History of the National Theatre* (London, 1978), 82.

42. The National Theatre, London. Courtesy the National Theatre of Great Britain.

Another major London project, the Barbican, offers yet another model of urban renewal utilizing the theatre as a central element (Fig. 43). The Barbican was intended to reclaim not a tenement area, but a large, heavily bombed district to the north of St. Paul's Cathedral. Its planned effect, however, was similar to that of Lincoln Center, as we may see in a London *Times* comment on the project in 1964: "Socially and architecturally this and other plans to bring a residential population back into the City are of the greatest significance, though the cost of land will lead to high rents."[38] In addition to upper-income housing (for some six thousand persons), the development includes schools and community buildings, and most notably an arts complex. England's "alternate" national theatre, the Royal Shakespeare Company, is now housed at the Barbican, and contributes significantly to the public image of this development.

[38] *Times* (London), November 17, 1964, 11.

43. The Barbican development. The Barbican theatre is marked with a T.
Courtesy Chamberlin, Powell, Bon, and Woods.

As these major civic monuments become incorporated into clusters
of other urban structures, however, the theatre begins to lose its architectural identity to that of the complex and the statement it makes as a
whole. Although the Vivian Beaumont Theatre stands somewhat apart
from the other structures at Lincoln Center, it visually functions as an
almost interchangeable unit of the group (and, indeed, tucked into a
back corner, is the least among equals.). The English National Theatre,
really several different theatre spaces housed in the same structure and
connected by common lobbies and (as at Lincoln Center) to other cultural monuments in the complex by open terraces, provides even less
of a sense of a distinct architectural unit. The Barbican Theatre is more
amorphous still. Completely contained within the Barbican development (the difficulty of finding it has been the source of jokes since its

opening), it is as remote architecturally from the great monumental theatres of the nineteenth century as were the equally enclosed theatrical spaces of the Renaissance court theatres. Indeed, with such theatrical spaces we have returned to a modern version of the early Renaissance theatres, with the supporting prince being replaced by real estate interests using the theatre as a cultural emblem for the enhancement of surrounding commercial property. This relationship is perfectly expressed in a development such as the Barbican, where the theatre is totally contained in the more significant development much the way the ducal theatres were enclosed in the palaces of their sponsors.

4

The Facade Theatre

Although examples of monumental theatres may today be found throughout the Western world, the public image of a physical theatre is much less likely in England or North America to be of a monumental structure than it is, for example, in Germany, where such theatres are much more common. Instead, the public of England or the United States is likely to think of a theatre as a contributing element to another major component in the modern city, the street facade.

The historical tension between the theatre as art form and the theatre as commercial enterprise has naturally been reflected in theatre structures and theatre locations. The monumental theatre, while rarely entirely devoid of commercial considerations, suggests, as we have seen, by its location and isolation, an affinity with other public cultural monuments. In this form the theatre is almost never found at or near the commercial center of a city, but more likely near elegant residential areas or surrounded by public parks and gardens. From the Renaissance onward, however, more commercially focused theatres have sought the business heart of the city, the marketplace, and have developed much closer architectural affinities to such commercial structures as banks and shops than to museums or churches, typically individualistic and isolated from the street facade row. Even before they had the advantage of permanent structures, medieval and early Renaissance companies set up their booths in the fairs and marketplaces alongside those of the purveyors of vegetables, chickens, clothing, and gingerbread.

In this temporary form the theatre aroused little protest, but when theatre troupes attempted to follow their market and fair neighbors in establishing more permanent commercial structures in the heart of the developing Renaissance cities, they met with great resistance. Europe's first permanent public theatre was established in Paris, toward the end of the fourteenth century, by a group of bourgeois who organized a religious society and decided to erect a theatre for the performance of passion plays. Paris at this time was one of the three largest cities in Europe (the other two were Venice and Milan), with a population of about 80,000. Its three traditional sections were already well established—the *cité*, the ancient heart of Paris, on an island in the Seine; the *université*, on the left (south) bank of the river; and the *ville*, on the north. A tithe record of 1352 shows that four fifths of the taxpayers and taxable wealth were located on the north bank, bisected by the major commercial artery, the Rue St.-Denis. The most elegant and popular developing neighborhoods were those at the east and west of the *ville*, near the royal residences—the Louvre in the west and the new Hôtel St.-Paul in the east.

Clearly the ideal location for a public theatre would have been the center of the prosperous *ville*, but the organizers apparently feared (correctly) that the municipality would not look with favor upon such an establishment. They erected their theatre instead in the small village of Saint-Maur, just to the east of Paris on the Vincennes road. The traditional boundary of the city was the fortified wall erected by Philippe Auguste early in the previous century, yet even before this wall was completed, settlements were springing up beyond it, among them Saint-Maur.

City officials began protesting the establishment of a permanent theatre structure soon after it opened, and a municipal decree of 1398 sought to extend city authority by forbidding the inhabitants of "Paris, Saint-Maur, and other towns around Paris" to perform any plays without the express leave of the prevost of Paris or the king. The actors appealed to the sovereign, Charles VI, however, and in a famous decree of 1402 he accorded them a patent, bestowing upon the company a political legitimacy which, as the document made clear, was confirmed by a geographical legitimacy as well. The company was henceforth permitted to perform in whatever location might establish "either in our city of Paris, or in the Prévosté, Viconté, or suburbs of it."[1] The company responded to this boon by moving almost at once to a location much nearer the commercial heart of the city, converting into a theatre a hall belonging to the Eglise de la Trinité on the Rue St.-Denis, not far to the north and west of the rapidly expanding central

[1]Louis Petit de Julleville, *Les mystères*, 2 vols. (Paris, 1880), 1:414–15, 417.

markets, Les Halles. Here they remained in evident prosperity for more than a century until a conversion of their quarters in 1547 forced them to find another, equally central location, contiguous to the central markets on the south.

The general urban arrangement of sixteenth-century London was in many ways similar to that of Paris: still essentially medieval, its official borders marked by ancient city walls on three sides. The Thames to the south provided a much clearer fourth boundary in London than did the Seine in Paris, because the far bank was only sparsely settled and no bridging element corresponding to Paris's Ile de la Cité existed. The population in London as in Paris grew rapidly during this century, but Henry VIII was not forced, unlike his contemporary, François I, to liquidate his own town houses or to approve the conversion of former dumping grounds and other unattractive locations for building sites to accommodate the pressures of expansion. The dissolution of the monasteries and ecclesiastical orders between 1536 and 1540 resulting from Henry's break with the Catholic church had placed under state control large areas of highly desirable land, much of which was soon freed for development. Elizabeth's ruling in 1580 that no new buildings could be constructed within three miles beyond the city walls, although only intermittently enforced, gave further encouragement to the development of these formerly ecclesiastic lands. Thus most of the major urban changes that occurred in London during this century, including the establishment of regular public theatres, were affected in some way or other by Henry's establishment of a national church.

Dramatic performances seem to have increased in number and popularity in London from the mid-1500s onward, but as in Paris, the city government viewed the theatre with considerable suspicion, and in 1575 the mayor and corporation banned actors from the city entirely. No royal decree appeared to counteract such antagonism, but the many ecclesiastic territories in and about the city provided theatre organizers with another kind of geographical opportunity. By 1575 a permanent theatre was apparently established for choir boys within the precincts of St. Paul's Cathedral, purportedly to rehearse entertainment for the court, but also to offer viewing of these "rehearsals" to a paying public. Since this ecclesiastic ground was under the jurisdiction not of the city but of the queen, who was willing to grant her protection, all attempts to close this theatre were thwarted.

In 1576 another theatre space was established in the territory of Blackfriars, which had been confiscated by the state in 1538 and turned to secular use. Parts of the property were rented, parts were used to store supplies for court spectacles. No longer a functioning ecclesiastical enclave like St. Paul's, it was nevertheless also a crown property and thus outside municipal jurisdiction. Such properties, called "liberties," were the most common locations for public theatres established in London during the following years. Even the theatres erected for the adult companies, whose greater size, more mixed public, and lesser influence at court made it impossible in these early years to move to such prize locations as St. Paul's or Blackfriars, gravitated toward the liberties on the more remote south bank of the Thames, assuming, correctly, that this would give them extra protection from local authorities. Here they joined other socially marginal establishments—bordellos and bear-baiting arenas—in what was essentially the first theatre district in modern times.

During the early seventeenth century, certain public theatres in London were able to move closer to the city center, though still within areas that for one reason or another were socially marginal. A royal charter of 1608 abolished the liberties but still exempted certain localities, most notably that around Whitefriars, from city taxes and maintainance. The Whitefriars inhabitants interpreted this ruling as placing them outside all municipal legislation, and the district, also known as Alsatia, became a notorious criminal sanctuary, as well as the location of several public theatres, including the Salisbury Court.

In Spain and Holland the early public theatres, better integrated into the social structure than these in England, appeared in more respectable locations in the urban structure as well. The *corrales* of Madrid and Seville were located in the very center of these cities, sometimes actually adjacent to aristocratic homes.[2] The first Dutch theatre, built by the Duytsche Academie in 1617, was located on the Keizergracht, a fashionable new residential street near the heart of Amsterdam. Like the *corrales* in Spain, the Academie was regarded by the authorities as more of an asset than an irritant, because both devoted a substantial percentage of their profits to charity, in the Dutch case the city orphanage.[3]

For the first commercial theatres located near town centers, finding a central and affordable space was usually the primary concern, and little attention was given to the facade presented to the street. Thus these theatres had little specific visual impact at first in the developing Renaissance cities. The wooden Amsterdam theatre was rebuilt in brick in 1637 with a handsome portico bearing in gold letters a verse of

[2]Hugo Rennert, *The Spanish Stage in the Time of Lope de Vega* (New York, 1963), 53.
[3]J. A. Worp, *Geschiedenis van den Amsterdamschen Schouwberg* (Amsterdam, 1920), 31.

Joost van den Vondel's calling for peace and tranquillity in the auditorium and banning pipe smoking, beer, and snacks inside,[4] but this sort of external elaboration was most unusual. Often, especially in early-seventeenth century France, public theatres were created by the conversion of previously existing spaces, halls or tennis courts, and little adjustment was made to the exterior of the structure beyond perhaps adding an identifying signboard, such as we see illustrated on the facade of the Hôtel de Bourgogne in the frontispiece to Georges de Scudéry's *Comédie des Comédiens* (Fig. 44).

Tennis courts, strictly utilitarian structures, rarely offered more to the street than a door and two or three windows, and were such undistinguished participants in the urban scene that when one Anthoine Loys petitioned the Parlement of Paris in 1602 for permission to erect such a structure, he was refused on two grounds: first, that the many such establishments already in the city contributed to the "debauching of youth," and second, that they added in no respect to the "ornament and decoration" of the capital.[5] Indeed the tennis courts often added nothing at all to the visual urban text, for many of them were built behind shops or combined shops and dwellings, to be reached by narrow passageways between other buildings. Nor was their being converted from these hidden tennis courts the only reason for the relative visual obscurity of many early public theatres. Even when new theatres were built, the most economical spaces for a structure necessarily much larger than a normal house or shop was often in the open space within the center of an urban block, with other buildings on all four sides, facing away toward surrounding streets. Access to the theatre might well be only a passageway between these pre-existing structures, with no opportunity offered for a distinctive facade even if the theatre builder had desired one. The Theatre Royal in Drury Lane was erected in a former riding yard, surrounded by other structures, and could be reached only by narrow streets, scarcely ten feet wide. Covent Garden, built nearby in 1733, was adjacent to the first great public square in London and one of the first in modern Europe, Inigo Jones's magnificent piazza, but it related in no evident way to that major public space, and like Drury Lane, could be reached only by narrow passageways (Fig. 45).

When the free-standing monumental theatres began to be constructed in Europe, external decoration necessarily became an impor-

---

[4]J. Fransen, *Les comédiens français en Hollande au XVIIe et au XVIIIe siècles* (Paris, 1925), 18.

[5]W. L. Wiley, *The Early Public Theatre in France* (Cambridge, Mass., 1960), 163.

44. Frontispiece of De Scudery's *Comédie des Comédiens*, 1635, showing the
entrance to the Hôtel de Bourgogne.

45. Part of Horwood's Plan of London (1799) showing Covent Garden and Drury Lane. Covent Garden in particular is almost

tant consideration, and although the isolation of such structures would have allowed all sides to be given equal decorative attention, in practice the placement of such buildings within the city, frequently at the end of vistas, particularly encouraged the use of a monumental facade, often derived from the same contemporary architectural vocabulary as those of other monumental structures. Thus the Dorset Garden theatre in London, an early forerunner of the monumental theatre, had a facade suggesting an elegant private residence (Fig. 46). This faced upon the river, to welcome its more elegant patrons who arrived by boat, since its actual physical surroundings were the disreputable area of Alsatia. The facades of the great monumental theatres of the late eighteenth century employed standard classic motifs and were virtually indistinguishable from other major public buildings of the period.

Although this generally rather severe style remained popular through the nineteenth century for public structures aimed to project an image of stability, tradition, and civic respectability, such as banks and court houses, the monumental theatre developed a more elaborate and baroque visual vocabulary, the outstanding example of which is the facade of Charles Garnier's Paris Opéra, composed of an almost overwhelming accumulation of cultural references (Fig. 47). We have already noted that the late-nineteenth-century opera house reflected in its physical location its assumption of a cultural role similar to that of the medieval cathedral, and what was true for location was true for decoration as well. The architect Robert Venturi has called the cathedral facade a "relatively two-dimensional screen for propaganda,"[6] and this is true also of the facade of a late-nineteenth-century opera house in the Garnier manner, the propaganda here, of course, being the ostentation of cultural rather than of religious iconography.

Through most of its history the monumental theatre has exemplified what Venturi calls the "decorated shed," to which external ornament is applied independent of interior function. This is even more true, however, of the theatre that presents itself to the urban public only as a single element in the facade streetscape of the modern city. The modern urban commercial block, comprising a row of contiguous facades, has been developed primarily to serve the needs of commerce. Potential customers move along the street as they moved along the rows of booths and stalls in the medieval market or as they move in present-day Middle Eastern souks, with each merchant displaying in his area a selection of attractive goods.

As markets gave way to permanent shopping streets merchants com-

---

[6]Robert Venturi, *Learning from Las Vegas* (Cambridge, Mass., 1972), 74.

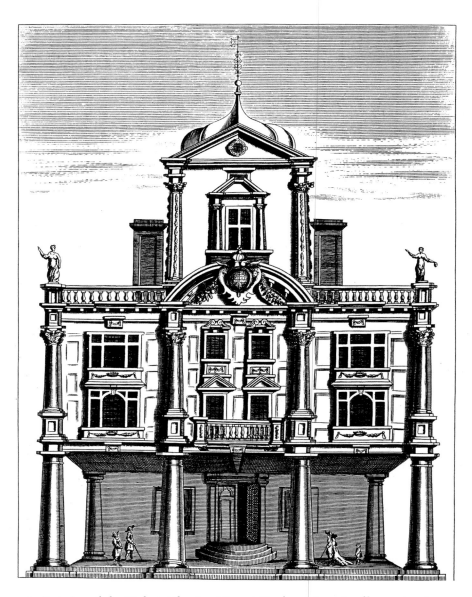

46. Exterior of the Duke's Theatre, Dorset Garden, 1673. An illustration from
Elkanah Settle's *The Empress of Morocco* (1673).

monly utilized their ground floor for a shop with, if possible, a display
window in the front, and lived on the floor or floors above. The most
valuable part of the structure was the ground-floor facade, where the
store made its critical contact with potential customers and attempted

47. The 1875 Paris Opéra, designed by Charles Garnier. Courtesy of the Bibliothèque National.

to attract them inside. The desirability of this commercial frontage meant that the establishments that could afford to do so took up as much ground-floor frontage as possible, but that the average building in a facade row was normally much deeper than it was wide, because of the intense competition for street frontage.

Probably no widely found element of the facade streetscape is so ill adapted to this particular spatial configuration as the modern commercial theatre. The long and narrow ducal theatres of the Renaissance would be the historical form best suited to such an arrangement, but their configuration, with few seats well situated for viewing the stage, would be quite unacceptable in a theatre seeking to attract a paying public. The most common auditorium shape when facade theatres were developing was a shallow or somewhat ovoid horseshoe, requiring a broad access space between auditorium and street. The result was that frequently the facade became almost literally the two-dimensional screen Venturi spoke of. It might be not even a wall of the theatre

proper but simply a public visual indication of a theatre's presence in the near vicinity, in fact giving access to a long passageway, as attractively decorated as the theatre could manage, leading to the actual theatre structure located, as it had often been from the seventeenth century onward, in the more open, inexpensive, and flexible space behind the neighboring stores.

This arrangement has often been used for facade theatres located on major thoroughfares where street space is in particularly high demand. At the beginning of the twentieth century, when Forty-second Street was booming, a facade on that street was so desirable that theatres (including the Liberty, the Lyric, and the Times Square) actually built on less fashionable and expensive Forty-first and Forty-third streets had extensions out to narrow facades to give them a Forty-second Street entrance. Ironically, with the decline in prestige and public image of Forty-second Street, these facades have become something of a liability, and theatres, when possible, have created other facades on the hitherto rejected but now less notorious parallel streets.

Even when the street facade was in fact a wall of the theatre itself, its shape, fenestration, and decoration almost never provided any information about the spaces inside or their use. The facade has instead generally served an essentially decorative function, attempting to present a particular public image for the attached theatre. Even this function is often fulfilled only with some difficulty, because of the close relationship between the facade theatre and its immediate environment. The monumental theatre's relationship to other structures in its area has often affected its design, but it is obviously far less susceptible to pressures to conform in some way to its neighbors than is the facade theatre, physically integrated into the urban streetscape. Whenever cities have developed facade rows, there has been tension between the desire to make the individual facades essentially identical, thus emphasizing the entire row as a visual unit, and the desire of the owners of each element to stress the individuality of their particular unit. The urban renovations of John Nash in London and Haussmann in Paris look toward the former goal, but for commercial structures such as stores or theatres the need to catch the eye of the passing citizen provides a strong counterforce.

Early facade theatres were as a rule integrated into their streetscapes with little attempt to suggest their specific function. At times, especially in quasi-residential areas, this lack of individuation seems to have owed something to a desire to defuse suspicions about so unusual a neighbor. The Paris Comédie of 1689 was built on a rather quiet side street after two locations had been refused by ecclesiastic authorities,

48. The Paris Comédie
Française in 1689. Courtesy
of the Bibliothèque
National.

and it offered a facade integrated entirely into its neighborhood, with
windows and balcony suggesting a private dwelling (Fig. 48). Its only
identification was a sign, and that a most indirect allusion to its activities—the goddess Minerva looking into the mirror of truth.[7] A
number of small public theatres located in similar areas during the
following century likewise sought to blend into their surroundings.

During the eighteenth and nineteenth centuries most facade theatres tended to follow the prevailing codes of facade decoration of the
period rather than to make use of elements that might specifically
identify them as theatres. The baroque idea of the planned city, reinforced by Cartesian rationalism, encouraged a vision of the streetscape
rather than the individual building as a visual unit, unless that building was set apart as an organizing focus. Continued arcades or repeated
patterns of columns and fenestration were used to impose a visual
rhythm along an entire row, whatever the functions of its individual
elements. This process was particularly evident when a single designer
controlled the plan for a large urban area, as Nash did in Regency
London and Haussmann in Second Empire Paris, but during the eighteenth century in particular, when a generalized neoclassic style was
widely employed for public and private buildings of any distinction,
the decorative motifs of theatres very often made their facades virtually indistinguishable from those of their neighbors even when a
specific overall street plan was not imposed on them.

[7]Emile Genest and E. Duberry, *La maison de Molière connue et inconnue* (Paris, 1922),
49.

London's Royalty Theatre (1787), for example, formed the center third of a typical carefully balanced eighteenth-century street composition (Fig. 49). The contemporary Théâtre National (1793) in Paris, later the home of the opera and possessing an interior disposition and decoration described by a historian as "of an extreme richness and grandeur," offered an exterior that "differed in no respect from the surrounding buildings, having only a portico of twelve arches stretching the entire length of the facade" (Fig. 50).[8]

During the nineteenth century urban facades became more varied, and individual commercial establishments, theatres included, were more likely to be differentiated in a facade row. Small facade theatres of this century still from time to time resembled private dwellings (as did New York's Grove Theatre, Fig. 51), and larger ones, especially in New York, might present a rather neutral facade with rows of similar windows giving an overall appearance little different from their urban neighbors. Indeed an English visitor in 1867 complained about the resulting "invisibility" of American places of entertainment. "With some few exceptions the American theatres are not distinguishable from the surrounding houses until a close proximity reveals the name, lights, and other outside paraphernalia of a place of amusement, for on either side the spacious entrance are usually to be found shops and above the windows of an hotel or retail store." So ambiguous or modest a public image would seem a serious disadvantage to an establishment dependent upon its ability to attract the attention of the passing public, but this visitor felt that the less obvious signs of its function displayed by the typical New York theatre were compensated for by the high concentration of theatres in a small area. "Unlike the system that exists in London of scattering the theatres, the plan adopted in New York has been to bring them as nearly as possible together, so that the overflow of one house finds another ready at hand."[9]

Here is suggested another standard feature of the facade theatre—its frequent appearance with other theatres of the same general type in a part of the city anthropologist Victor Turner might have characterized as a "liminoid" district, an area of entertainment and recreation where citizens go for a variety of experiences set apart from the concerns of everyday life. This liminoid quality gives to districts of this sort a special excitement, often with a distinctly raffish or risqué element. The urban companions of facade theatres have not traditionally been such elements as banks, major office buildings, or large stores, but

---

[8]Adolphe Jullien, "Les salles de l'Opéra de 1671 à 1873," *Revue de France* 8 (1873), 447.
[9]Quoted in Mary Henderson, *The City and the Theatre* (Clifton, N.J., 1973), 121.

Published as the Act directs June 4 1787 and Sold only by C Brady at the Theatre.

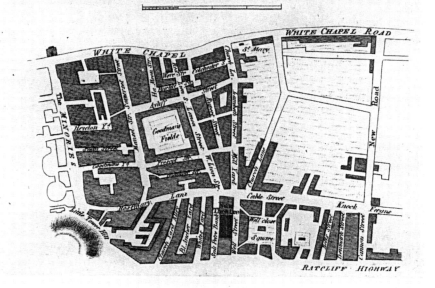

ROYALTY THEATRE.

49. The Royalty Theatre in London, 1787. It is the dark rectangle near the bottom of the map. Courtesy of the Harvard Theatre Collection.

50. The Théâtre National (Théâtre des Arts), Paris, 1793. Courtesy of the
Bibliothèque National.

rather other leisure establishments—cafés, hotels, small specialty (especially souvenir) stores, and less culturally respectable competing entertainments—panoramas and vaudevilles, menageries, burlesque houses, wax museums, freak shows, and more recently, cinemas. Sexual titillation has almost always been a part of the stimulus of such areas, and a variety of establishments of different degrees of respectability have normally played their part in providing the district's particular ambiance. Easy access by mass transportation has also been essential to such districts in modern times, and a convergence of major bus, train, or subway lines today almost always is found in such a district.

The first European city to contain several facade theatres was Paris, and it is significant that they established themselves at once in a rather restricted area, which became, by the opening of the nineteenth century, the first modern entertainment district, the Boulevard du Temple (Fig. 52). Haussmann's rebuilding of the city during the Second Empire removed the center of this district but encouraged its development westward along his new boulevards. By the early twentieth century, in addition to locations along the boulevards (the French still speak of the offerings of these houses as "boulevard drama"), facade theatres had

51. The 1804 Grove Theatre, New York. Courtesy of the Harvard Theatre Collection.

52. Panorama of the Boulevard du Temple in Paris from the Gaîté theatre to the Rue d'Angoulême, about 1830. The Funambules and Délassements-Comiques theatres are the third and fourth facades from the left. Edmond Auguste Texier, *Tableaux de Paris* (1852).

established a focal area in the vicinity of the new Opéra, an area where the number of theatres has steadily increased during this century.

The clustering of New York commercial theatres noted by the mid-nineteenth-century English visitor has been a feature of that city almost from the beginning, and since the early 1800s has followed a quite predictable pattern, moving steadily up Broadway and locating successively around each of the special intersections created by this boulevard's crossing of other major streets—first Park Row, then Canal, then Fourteenth (Union Square). As the city expanded to the north, each time Broadway, moving diagonally, crossed one of the north-south avenues, it formed what the New York planners call a bow-tie intersection, two long open triangles touching at their tips. During the later nineteenth century the theatre district continued its northward movement, in the words of Tony Hiss, writing in *The New Yorker*, "lighting up one bow tie after another: Union Square in the eighteen-sixties, Madison Square in the eighties, Herald Square in the Gay Nineties,"[10] and Times Square at the turn of the century (Fig. 53).

In London the licensing act discouraged the sort of proliferation of commercial theatres seen in New York and Paris and thus the developing of a distinct theatre district where such enterprises clustered, but

[10]Tony Hiss, "Reflections," *The New Yorker*, June 29, 1987, 77.

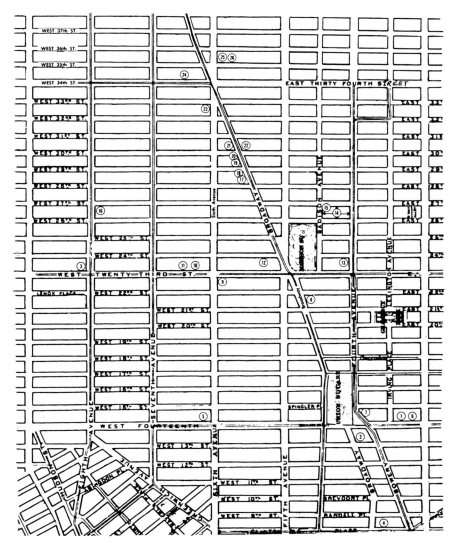

53. Locations of New York theatres in the late nineteenth century. The Union Square Theatre (no. 7) should be on the south side of Fourteenth Street, between Broadway and the Bowery. Courtesy Mary C. Henderson.

even so the 1867 English visitor somewhat exaggerated the difference. The areas around Drury Lane, Covent Garden, and especially the parts of the Strand nearest to them have been recognized since the Restoration as London's major theatre district. By the 1860s even Soho, Haymarket, and St. James were hardly the remote and "secluded byways" this visitor called them; rather, they were the developing western edges of the city, not dissimilar in fact to New York's Fourteenth and Twenty-third streets where at this same time American entrepreneurs were erecting seemingly rather remote theatres, anticipating correctly that as the city grew the entertainment district would move in this direction.

An important part of modern theatre history has involved smaller, experimental theatres that have often appeared in the urban text as facade theatres, though of a much more modest type than the regular commercial houses. Like the larger facade theatres, these are often found near one another, but rarely in the sort of entertainment districts where the larger theatres are located (although perhaps on the very edges of such districts). The expense of such locations is obviously an important consideration, but so is the position of the experimental theatre in theatrical culture as a whole. The basis of its audience is not the same as that of the standard commercial theatres of Broadway and the West End but rather a more specialized public often involved with or strongly interested in experimentation in the other arts as well. Thus such theatres have often tended to appear not in hotel and entertainment districts, but in areas associated with contemporary artists, their studios, and galleries. So one found in early-twentieth-century Paris a cluster of minor theatres in Montmartre and Montparnasse (some of them still in operation); the off-Broadway theatres of New York, though located in many parts of the city, were concentrated in the early years of the movement in Greenwich Village around Sheridan Square and gradually moved to the east and south as the center of the New York painting scene shifted in those directions.

The boulevard theatres in Paris were the first regularly to offer facades setting them apart from their neighbors; by the late nineteenth century facade theatres elsewhere in Europe and in America generally followed this pattern. They followed the French theatres in general style of facade decoration, too, almost invariably utilizing elements of the classical architectural reprtoire, displaying highly eclectic blends of columns, pilasters, pediments, balustrades, niches with statuary, urns, and palladian windows, as if to bear witness to the cultural respectability of the establishment (Fig. 54).

In the early nineteenth century a few theatres, such as the Bowery in New York, went directly to the Greek temples for a model, with the result that their facades made a jarringly anachronistic note in the streetscape. Significantly, a number of early engravings of the Bowery sought to deny this visual effect by portraying the theatre as an isolated monument, which it never was, or even simply as an etherialized facade surrounded by clouds (Fig. 55). Nash's Haymarket theatre in

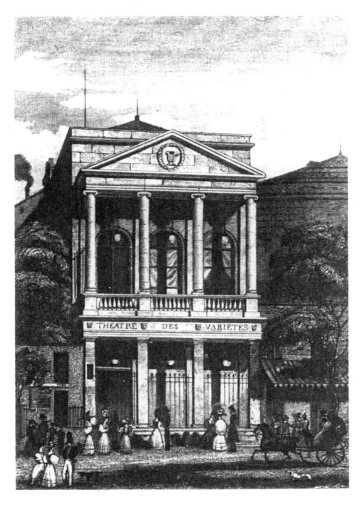

54. The Variétés, Paris. A typical late-nineteenth-century boulevard theatre. Courtesy of the Bibliothèque National.

London, with a massive columned portico, made a similarly obtrusive statement, but Nash was seeking to gain much of the effect of a monumental theatre in this facade house, and its relationship to its neighbors was of much less importance to him than its usefulness as a landmark in the district as a whole. Thus, instead of remodeling the existing theatre of that name, he built an entirely new one immediately to the south so that its facade could terminate the vista leading up Charles Street from fashionable St. James's Square (Fig. 56).

The more common pattern of classic facade, that established by the

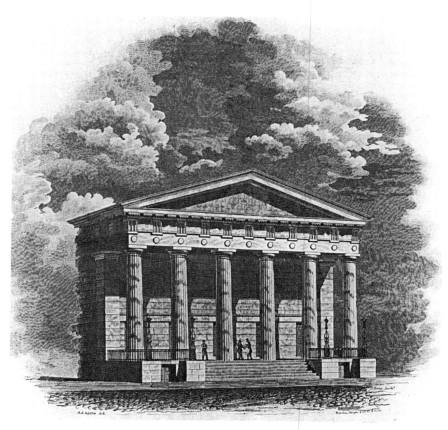

55. Facade of the Bowery Theatre, New York. Contemporary engraving, courtesy of the Theatre Collection of the Museum of the City of New York.

Parisian boulevard theatres at the end of the eighteenth century, was normally tall and narrow, sometimes the width of a narrow auditorium, but more frequently the width of a conventional street frontage, giving access to a vestibule leading to the theatre proper, hidden away deeper in the city block. Only a few theatres were able to afford a longer facade along the valuable boulevard space, the sort called for if the actual side of the theatre, for example, were placed there. Despite an enormous variety in decorative detail, the theatres in this most common architectural facade tradition have followed quite consistent overall decorative arrangements from their first appearance until recent times. The facade is normally divided into three horizontal units, the lowest containing entrances, and often little else, the second containing the most impressive architectural elaboration, based upon windows, arches, columns, and pilasters, and the third offering much more

56. Nash's Haymarket Theatre from Charles Street. The former theatre is the
less imposing and less advantageously located structure to the left of Nash's
building. Edwin Beresford Chancellor, *The Pleasure-Haunts of London* (1925).

modest fenestration, often topped by a pediment or other roof element.
In facade theatres of the late eighteenth and early nineteenth centuries
the middle unit was almost invariably the most ornate, making the
strongest architectural statement, and when the theatre displayed a
title or emblem it was normally located there. The two most common
arrangements for this space were a colonnade, a row of ornate windows, or a combination of the two, usually three arched windows and
four columns. In London, Paris, and New York (especially during the
era when the Times Square–Forty-second Street theatres were built),
these arrangements were so common as to identify the building possessing them, with reasonable certainty, as a theatre, even if it possessed no specific external sign (Fig. 57).

The functional styles of the interwar years and the glass walls of
more modern times have influenced recent facade theatre construc-

57. The present Belasco Theatre, New York, 1907. Courtesy of the Theatre Collection of the Museum of the City of New York.

tion, but the basic stock of theatres in major theatre cities is still found in the entertainment districts, now showing a bit of age, established around the turn of the century, and the majority of theatre structures in these districts still reflect the fashionable architectural codes, especially French neoclassic, which were favored for commercial theatres at that time.

The major function of such facades clearly went beyond identifying a building as a theatre. Their primary purpose was rather to reinforce a certain desired public image. Just as the columned porticos of the nineteenth-century bank and law court attempted to project an image of solidity and civic power, and the gothic traceries of the nineteenth-century church the tradition of the faith, so the classical/baroque compositions of the facade theatre were intended to suggest high elegance and refined culture.

For the more mundane matter of attracting an audience to a specific building, the theatre generally relied on temporary lights, billboards, and posters to call the attention of the passerby, and the employment of such signifying elements is often the most striking and distinctive feature of facade theatres. The applied ornament at street level and often above, a more direct and practical sort of signification than the architectural features, frequently indeed quite obscures the latter.

Changes in theatre-going and production habits are often clearly reflected in the design and utilization of these temporary signs. Regular theatre-goers during much of the nineteenth century knew that they could generally find a fairly predictable sort of entertainment at certain theatres, performed by a familiar company of actors, and would often seek out those theatres rather than any specific production. Thus the name of the production was generally given only modest attention on the theatre facade, while the largest sign (sometimes the only one) was the name of the theatre. This almost universal practice, it might be noted, is quite different from that of monumental theatres, which do not display their names on their exteriors, partly because they are meant to be recognizable in themselves as monuments, and partly because they are not in competition with any other similar structures nearby so that differentiation is necessary. On the rare occasions when a monumental theatre bears an external inscription, that inscription is likely to be a motto of some sort, reflecting national, cultural, or artistic values—"Art to the People" on the original Berlin Volksbühne and "Liberty, Fraternity, Equality—or Death" on the French national theatre during the Revolution.

Major projecting elements on facade theatres were uncommon until the later nineteenth century (and are still much more common in North America and England than elsewhere). Typically the name of the theatre was incised into the facade itself at an upper level. Other permanent linguistic signs, if there were any, most commonly indicated the various entrances (the boxes, pit, and gallery of English theatres, for example) or the function of the structure (drama, music). The title of the particular performance was often indicated on temporary placards or painted boards placed near the entrances. With the establishment of the modern production system emphasizing the long run (a phenomenon much more closely associated with the commercially oriented facade theatres than with the civic monumental theatres), the custom of going to a particular theatre was replaced by that of going to a particular play, so that today even many persons who rarely if ever attend the theatre probably know the names of certain long-running plays or musicals but few, even among those who have attended these performances, are likely to know the name of the theatres where they are housed. This change in public image has naturally been reflected in the embellishment of the facade, where the title of the play inside, for example, *Cats* or *Les Misérables*, now occupies a far more prominent position than the name of the theatre, and indeed sometimes replaces it.

Early-nineteenth-century facade theatres, unlike monumental houses, had little in the way of porticos, at most only a small roofed area extending to the street for those wealthier patrons alighting from carriages. By the end of the century, when intermissions had become almost universal and theatres (especially in New York, where lobby spaces tend to be smaller than in Europe) felt the need of a larger outdoor covered area, the modern marquee, extending on the street level for most of the width of the facade, became a standard element. This provided another area for display of signs and was soon so used (Fig. 58).

At the beginning of the twentieth century, a transitional period when the names of theatres and those of productions received almost equal emphasis on the typical facade, the theatre's name was commonly placed on the two sides of the marquee, built permanently into it, with a changing production name beneath. This practice, now rarely seen in live theatres, has been much more consistently followed in film theatres, and the illustrated sign, with the title of the theatre permanently above and the present film in temporary letters beneath, has become an instantly recognizable feature of the cinema facade. Because film intermissions are extremely rare, no need for external shelter exists, and these signs have therefore been reduced to their functional minimum, often merely a projecting triangle over the entrance, allowing maximum visibility from both sides of the sign.

Although a few extant facade theatres have their names incised high on the facade in the manner favored during the past century, the more common practice today is to display the name of the theatre on a protruding sign in this same area, which has greater visibility from the street. Methods of displaying the title of the production vary from country to country. In Paris it is normally rather modestly displayed, often only on posters found flanking the theatre's main entrance. In London and New York, it generally appears on a sign much larger than that identifying the theatre, usually placed just above the marquee (Fig. 59).

Other, auxiliary signs, featuring favorable phrases from reviews or

58. Facade of the Ritz Theatre, New York. Courtesy of the Theatre Collection of the Museum of the City of New York.

information about prizes the production has won, often supplement this large sign, and may be hung from the marquee, posted next to the doors, or displayed on boards in front of the theatre. The prominence of these review quotations, a recent development in facade theatre decoration, accurately if unfortunately reflects the profound dependence of the present commercial theatre upon the reviewer, but equally revealing is the emphasis given to the title of the production. In many theatres, especially those featuring musicals, which have major name recognition and when they are successful, extremely long runs, the title may cover most of the facade and quite overwhelm all other information. The importance of such signs is indicated not only by their relative size, but, especially in New York, by their orientation. Most of the so-called Broadway theatres are in fact not located on Broadway, but instead on the streets on either side, primarily between

59. An early example of the large production sign: *Desire under the Elms* at the Earl Carroll Theatre, New York. Notice the layout of the sign. Courtesy of the Theatre Collection of the Museum of the City of New York.

Forty-third and Fiftieth streets. Broadway nevertheless is the obvious entertainment artery and patrons heading for a theatre on foot are most likely to approach it from that direction. The vast majority of these will already have purchased tickets, the predominantly walk-in public being a phenomenon long disappeared. But partly in hope of last-minute sales and partly in provide guidance for patrons already planning to attend, the major theatres orient their signs, like sunflowers, to the glow of Broadway. Thus a pedestrian looking west on a street like Forty-fifth from Broadway will see a great number of display signs angled out from facades that cannot be seen, while someone looking down this same block from Eighth Avenue, the opposite direction, will receive little such information (Fig. 60). The same practice, though on a much smaller scale, may be seen on London's Shaftesbury Avenue and Charing Cross Road. What is thus displayed, in every case, is of course not the name of the theatre, but the production offered there, a far more relevant piece of information for the contemporary theatre-goer.

The facade display of the smaller off-Broadway theatres is naturally more modest, though for the most well established of these theatres, it follows many of the same codes. During the 1960s theatres throughout Greenwich Village adopted the practice of identifying themselves with large banners projecting into the street from the upper floors of the facade, so that a particular building could be recognized as a theatre even from a block or two away (Fig. 61). Such banners for theatres are today almost extinct (though they are now often used by Village shops and by Soho art galleries); indeed, many of the more recent off-off Broadway theatres seem to take pride (like certain of the most exclusive New York restaurants) in providing little or no information about their function on the facade. La Mama, one of the best known and most influential of the experimental theatres of New York, has always avoided any signs of its activity on its facade.

This official invisibility has become a common feature in the new experimental theatres of the East Village, as may be seen in the physical descriptions of a number of such theatres in a 1985 special issue of *The Drama Review* devoted to them: "Without the street number the club would be impossible to find" (Club Chandalier). "The only beacons are some unobtrusive spray-painted letters over a brick wall and the number 118 in black" (Darinka). "There is little to identify the theatre from the outside except a small sign on the wall above the door saying 'Limbo.' Otherwise it looks pretty much like the other tenements and storefronts of the neighborhood" (Limbo Lounge). "There is no name, no sign—except for a black-outlined, stacked stone pyramid painted over the door" (Pyramid Club). "To find the theatre it is helpful to know the address, since the storefront that houses it does not call attention to itself—there is no sign on the building indicating that it is a theatre" (WOW Cafe).[11] As Michael Kirby observes in his introduc-

[11]Jill Dolan, et al., "An Evening in the East Village," *The Drama Review* 29 (Spring 1985), 27, 32, 39, 44, 50.

60. Forty-fifth Street in New York (1988), looking west from Broadway, and showing Broadway-oriented signs. The huge booted leg overhanging the facade in the distance is a metonymic representation of the Giant in Sondheim's *Into the Woods*, playing in this theatre. Photo by Lynn Doherty.

61. The banner of the Circle Repertory Theatre in Sheridan Square (1988), one of the few theatre banners still flying in Greenwich Village. Photo by Lynn Doherty.

62. The entrance to Darinka (behind the bicycle), 118 East First Street, New York (1985). Photo by Michael Kirby. Courtesy *The Drama Review*.

tion to this issue, such theatre is "closely tied to the place in which it is created and the socio-cultural milieu from which it is generated,"[12] and its integration into its neighborhood is signified by its assimilated facade. These theatres, like other small experimental theatres in Europe, serve a small and intimate public, who know where the theatrical event is taking place and need no external information (Fig. 62). Indeed the absence of external signs reinforces feeling of intimacy, exclusiveness, and focus on the internal event, and creates, as a result of all of this, a conscious and striking contrast to the traditional commercial house with its flashing lights, billboards, and lavish displays of quotes from favorable reviews.

[12]Michael Kirby, "East Village Performance," *The Drama Review* 29 (Spring 1985), 4.

5

Interior Space

In the preceding chapters we have considered theatre structures and spaces as elements within various urban arrangements and explored some of the many ways such elements have been utilized at different periods and in different cultures. The meaning involved in such matters as location and exterior decoration are of course available to all members of a community, whether they attend the theatre or not. We now turn to consider those messages available only to the theatre's own public, the messages involved in spaces and decorations within the theatre structure.

Many discussions of architectural semiotics begin with a consideration of space, and this is hardly surprising. Architecture might almost be defined as the creation of a specific articulation of space; indeed, some recent architectural semioticians in Paris have argued that the semiotics of architecture might be more properly regarded as part of a more general semiotics of space, while others in Naples have called the internal space the "signified" of a building rather than simply one of its various morphological features. Whatever its more specialized functions, it is primarily "about space."

The articulation of space is a phenomenon of particular importance to the theatre as a cultural system, since a certain spatial configuration is so basic to this system that it can almost be taken as a defining condition of theatre, even in the absence of *any* specific architectural structure. This configuration is suggested by the word "theatre" itself—a place where one observes. Many theorists and historians have stressed as central to theatre the implied dialectic of the space of the observer and the space of the observed. Richard Southern in *The Seven Ages of Theatre* proposes to "peel off" the various "accretions" the theatre has accumulated during the centuries. At the essential core thus discovered he finds two separate but linked pieces, the Player and the Audience. "Take these apart and you have nothing left."[1]Eric Bentley's "minimal definition" of theatre involves the same configuration: "A impersonates B while C looks on."[2] David Cole's anthropological approach brings us to the same dialectical relationship by a different route. For Cole, theatre occurs in a mystic place created by the confrontation of two worlds—the uncanny, dangerous, and fascinating space of the archetypical *illus tempus* inhabited by our representative shaman/actor and the duller and safer world of everyday reality from which we observe him. It is not these separate spaces for player and observer which make theatre, but their simultaneous presence and confrontation: "*As against* the Actor, we take on the collective character of the Audience."[3]

This particular spatial relationship thus characterizes theatre even when it is not enclosed in a physical structure, and it sets theatre apart from spatial organizations employed in other cultural systems, few of them so consistent in this matter as the theatre. Every culture has its own systems for the arrangement of space within a dwelling, for example, but the dwelling has no general cross-cultural relationship of spaces corresponding to the basic code of theatre, nor do the structures of commerce, despite the dialectic relationship of buyer and seller. The church or temple has perhaps the closest systematic architectural relationship to the theatre, since it involves the meeting of a secular celebrant with a sacred celebrated, but the sacred may be only spiritually or symbolically present, not spatially, as a player must be. Certain religious structures, such as the traditional Quaker meeting house, are thus able to avoid the setting aside of a "sacred" space within their confines. Without a player's space, however, there would be no theatre.

Among the "axioms for an environmental theatre," Richard Schechner has claimed that "actor and audiences employ the same space,"[4] but this is not precisely the case. The dream of Rousseau, and later of Adolphe Appia, Antonin Artaud, and others, of a theatre in which no distinction is made between actor and spectator, has inspired an important segment of twentieth-century experimentation and has led to

---

[1]Richard Southern, *The Seven Ages of Theatre* (New York, 1961), 2.

[2]Eric Bentley, *The Life of the Drama* (New York, 1964), 150.

[3]David Cole, *The Theatrical Event: A "Mythos," a Vocabulary, a Perspective* (Middletown, Conn., 1975), 71.

[4]Richard Schechner, "6 Axioms for Environmental Theatre," *The Drama Review* 12 (Spring 1968), 43.

frequent abandonment of the long-established stage/audience spatial confrontation, but even when no *specific* space is set aside for players in such events, anyone who has been in an audience sharing apparently the same physical space as performing actors will have felt the tenacity of Cole's description: the actor remains an uncanny, disturbing "other," inhabiting a world with its own rules, like a space traveler within a personal capsule, which the audience, however physically close, can never truly penetrate.

Though this essential spatial dialectic remains a constant, the location, size, shape, and exact relationship of the actor and audience spaces have naturally changed according to changing ideas about the function of theatre and its relationship to other cultural systems. One might arrange these relationships in a spectrum from the entirely separate, as in the nineteenth century picture-frame stage with an imaginary or even a literal screen dividing the two spaces, to the highly integrated, as in Schechner's environmental theatre, where each performer may have only a private "pocket" of performance space. If one pulls together these "pockets" to form a single actor space in the midst of an audience, one moves toward an arena form, the most integrated form with clearly separate actor/audience spaces. This is a natural arrangement for an otherwise undifferentiated space and is often found in theatrical performances created outside of specific physical structures.

The Greek theatre in all probability began as an arena, but at the beginning of the classical period added another element to the repertoire of theatrical spaces which was to have enormous importance and widely varied uses in subsequent periods. The use of slightly modified hillsides as seating areas had already begun the practice of gathering the audience around one side of the performance space or orchestra. In the early fifth century, a structure called the skene house was erected on the side of the orchestra across from the audience to provide an "offstage" space for actors to change costumes and masks and to furnish rapid and easy entrances to the acting area. Thus to the basic actor/audience spaces was added a third auxiliary space for the actors, a major elaboration that historically and geographically has been the most widespread of the spatial modifications on the basic confronting spaces.

In *Eléments de sémiologie*, Barthes suggested that in human society practically nothing escapes semiotization. Any object created or used almost at once assumes signifying functions in addition to strictly utilitarian ones: "As soon as there is a society, it converts every usage into a sign of that usage."[5] Thus, for example, a garment created to protect its wearer from rain becomes almost at once also a sign for specific atmospheric conditions. In the Greek skene house both utilitarian and signifying functions seem to have been present from the very beginning. A number of recent theorists have discussed the central preoccupation of the theatre with hiding and showing and with presence and absence.[6] The skene house, in addition to its practical service, provided a tangible sign for the hidden "other" world of the actor, the place of appearance and disappearance, the realm of events not seen but whose effects conditioned the visible world of the stage. Certain theatres, especially Eastern ones, have emphasized this "otherwordly" semiotic of backstage areas. In the classical Sanskrit theatre, for example, the voices of the gods traditionally are heard from this area.[7]

Aside from philosophically representing the other, hidden world that it was created to offer practically, the skene house from the beginning, as semiotized objects tend to do, took on a variety of secondary levels of meaning. In its first known appearance, in Aeschylus' *Oresteia*, the skene was offered as a representation of the palace at Thebes and later as the temple of Apollo. Its main door became the door of these structures, as well as a display area for scenic tableaux drawn from the hidden world of its interior. Its walls, probably with the aid of painted panels, iconically represented temple and palace walls, its roof city walls, palace roofs, even the abode of the gods.

Even in the simple trestle stages of the popular theatre from the classical period onward this same combination of functions may be observed. Behind the acting area is a curtain that serves on a utilitarian level to mask backstage areas, but by usage and decoration it converts those areas symbolically into the fictive offstage world (Fig. 63). In the earliest printed editions of Terence, slots in this curtain have signs above them indicating that they are to be taken as doorways into bedchambers or into individual houses (Fig. 64). The English Renaissance theatre, a permanent structure, may still have used a curtain at the rear of its acting area, but it also had a variety of permanent doors and balconies that could represent various locations. Sir Philip Sidney

[5]Roland Barthes, *Elements of Semiology*, trans. Annette Lavers and Colin Smith (New York, 1968), 41.

[6]See, for example, Herbert Blau, "Universals of Performance; or Amortizing Play," *Sub-stance* 37–38 (1983), and Michael Goldman, *The Actor's Freedom* (New York, 1975), 35–38.

[7]A. B. Keith, *The Sanskrit Theatre* (Oxford, 1924), 359.

63. Renaissance farce performance on a temporary stage. Detail of Pieter Balten, *The Performance of the Farce "Een cluyte van Plaeyerwater."* Courtesy of the Rijksmuseum.

mentions *Thebes* "written in great letters upon an old doore."[8] As the modern proscenium theatre developed, and the stage area came increasingly commonly to represent a room interior, the rear wall, which in exterior theatres most often was taken to represent a masked interior, came conventionally to represent access to a fictive exterior.

Perhaps as early as the Greek theatre and certainly in the later classical period another theatrical supporting space appeared, which supplemented the spectators' area somewhat as the backstage space supplemented the actors'. Each served as a transitional space between the outside world, where actors and audience might mingle in different

[8]Sir Philip Sidney, "An Apologie for Poetrie," in J. H. Smith and E. W. Parks, eds., *The Great Critics* (New York, 1951), 216.

64. Scene on a Renaissance Terence-Stage, showing performance of *Andria*. From the Lyons edition of the works of Terence, 1493.

relationships, and the special dialectic world of the stage and auditorium. Both actors and spectators use these intermediate spaces to prepare themselves for their different "roles" in the central confrontational space. In the backstage areas, actors get into costume and makeup and ready themselves physically and psychologically for their upcoming contact with the audience. In their lobbies and foyers the spectators make more modest but parallel adjustments. In a modern theatre they may check their coats, chat with others preparing to share the same experience, read programs and perhaps posted reviews, and generally remove themselves, as these spaces encourage them to do, from their extratheatrical concerns. At intermissions, both actors and spectators retire to their separate support spaces, where both may relax briefly with their fellows from the tensions and obligations of the performance. By tradition, each support space is off-limits to the inhabitants of the other, and those rare occasions when spectators have been permitted to invade backstage areas or when actors have appeared in lobbies and foyers have usually had about them an aura of transgression and the breaking of normal cultural codes. Modern experimental directors concerned with such matters as the attempted establishment of a closer community between actors and audience have often recognized the semiotic power of this division and sought to overcome it. Schechner and French experimental director Ariane Mnouchkine have invited audiences to arrive before the performance and come "backstage" to witness the actors' preparations. Andrei Serban's *Fragments of a Trilogy* begins among the spectators in the lobby. Indeed in certain experimental theatres the lobby seems to be losing its traditional function as an essentially neutral transitional space between external world and auditorium and is becoming an antechamber to the performance space, housing actual performance elements. French critics have begun to speak of the "politique d'accueil" (politics of welcome), in which the semiotics of the performance situation are extended to meet the audience in what has been traditionally exclusively an audience space.

Both support spaces have also traditionally been subdivided according to general spatial codes found in various forms in a wide variety of architectural systems, according to which social status is signified by more impressive and more centrally or conveniently located space. Thus in the traditional Western theatre of the nineteenth and twentieth centures, the leading actors have been given private dressing rooms or even small suites located near the stage, while performers of lower status move down the spatial scale into smaller and shared spaces, less conveniently situated, and often accessible only by stairs. The prevailing system at the end of the nineteenth century is spelled out in some detail in one of a series of articles on theatre design in the *Building News and Engineering Journal*:

> Like everything else in a theatre, there must be much division, and subdivision, even among the dressing rooms—first for the purposes of safety and fireproof construction, and secondly for the separation and classification of the performers. . . . The lady or gentleman who plays the leading parts *must* have a dressing room exclusively for herself or himself; the room must be capable of division by curtain or otherwise into two parts, to serve as a reception-room or boudoir, and dressing room respectively and . . . be capable of the fashionable decoration of the time, whatever that may be.[9]

[9]Ernest Woodrow, "Theatres," *Building News and Engineering Journal*, July 14, 1893, 38.

The semiotic importance of the dressing room is as clearly understood by a modern actor as that of the size and position of his or her
name on the theatre marquee or in the advertisements, and may similarly be a key concern in contracts or verbal negotiations. Alan
Schneider tells of an actress who gave two weeks notice of quitting a
production the afternoon of its opening upon discovering that she had
been assigned not the fifth dressing room, which she had expected, but
the sixth.[10]

Audience spaces have almost always reflected with great accuracy
the class preoccupations of their society. The ancient Greek auditorium has often been cited as a model of "democratic" seating and
indeed was considerably less socially organized than most subsequent
Western theatre seating. It did, however, accord privileged spaces in
the first row to public officials and priests, who were provided in some
theatres with stone seats bearing their names. Foreigners and late-
comers were apparently accommodated in the somewhat inferior outer
wedges of the great semicircle of seats. The major part of the seating
was spatially coded in any case at least in the great theatre at Athens,
where the center section behind the priest of Dionysius was seemingly
reserved for guests of honor, while each of the Athenian tribes occupied its own wedge of seating (Fig. 65).[11] Certain later indoor theatres looked back to this Greek model with its democratic connotations, most notably the Teatro Olimpico at Vicenza during the
Renaissance and Wagner's nineteenth-century Festspielhaus at Bayreuth.

The Olimpico organization of audience space was unique among
Renaissance theatres, suggesting, as George Kernodle has remarked, its
function as the theatre of a "club of equals" rather than of a princely
court (Fig. 66). Here all seats were of approximately equal importance
and the stage was provided with multiple perspectives "to make each
of the spectators feel as important as a prince."[12] Sebastiano Serlio, in
one of the first Renaissance treatises to deal with the construction of a
space for theatre, suggested how even the democratic seating of classical times could be adjusted to reflect the social divisions required in
modern audience arrangements (Fig. 67). In his adaptation of it to the
interior of a great hall, he kept the semicircular orchestra of the late

[10]Alan Schneider, *Entrances* (New York, 1986), 202.
[11]Margerete Bieber, *The History of the Greek and Roman Theatre* (Princeton, 1961),
71.
[12]George Kernodle, *From Art to Theatre* (Chicago, 1944), 170.

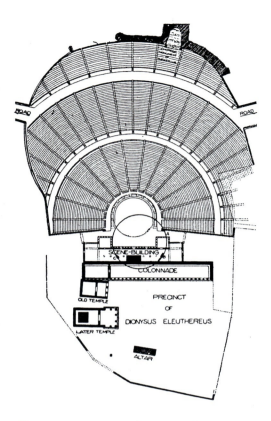

65. Ground plan of the precinct
of Dionysus Eleuthereus in
Athens after the construction of
the first stone theatre (c. 332–326
B.C.). From Roy C. Flickinger, *The
Greek Theatre and Its Drama*
(1918).

Greek theatre, ringing it with seats reserved for the most honored
guests, as indeed the Athenians had done, but his further subdivisions
reflect the social concerns of his own society:

> The first tiers, which are marked G, are for the most noble ladies; the
> ladies of lesser rank are placed higher up. The broader levels marked H
> and I are passageways between which are tiers reserved for the noble-
> men. Men of lesser rank will sit on the tiers above. The large space
> marked K is for the common people and may vary in size according to
> the dimensions of the hall.[13]

Perhaps the most important single feature of the Renaissance theatre
was the enormous symbolic influence of perspective in it. The almost
universal arrangement was not that of the Olimpico, but of such subse-

[13]Sebastiano Serlio, *The Second Book of Architecture*, trans. Allardyce Nicoll, in *The
Renaissance Stage*, ed. Barnard Hewitt (Coral Gables, Fla., 1958), 22–24.

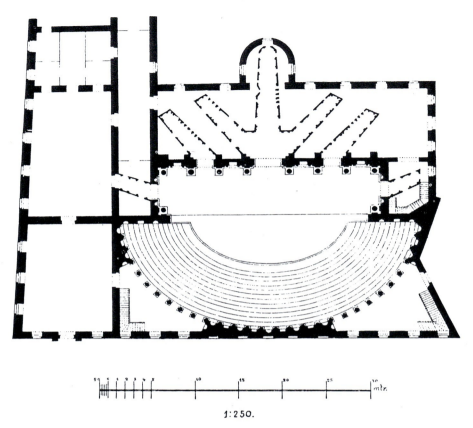

66. Ground plan of the Teatro Olimpico, Vicenza, 1584. *Theatre Arts*, 1921.

quent theatres as the Gonzaga theatre at Sabbioneta, the Medici theatre in Florence, and the Farnese theatre in Parma. In these theatres a
major shift in spatial organization occurred. To the extent that any
audience area was favored in seating arrangements among the Greeks,
it was those seats closest to the acting area, but the first perspective
theatre drawings, by Serlio and others, were oriented for a far higher
ideal spectator, clearly removed from the performance area. Similarly,
Sabbioneta's designer, Vincenzo Scamozzi, and his followers moved
the privileged audience space to an elevated central position in the
auditorium, where the sponsoring prince could look down upon his
assembled subjects as well as provide a visual anchor for the stage
perspective.

The one-point system of perspective became increasingly established in the theatre along with the spatial commitment to a single

Interior Space　**137**

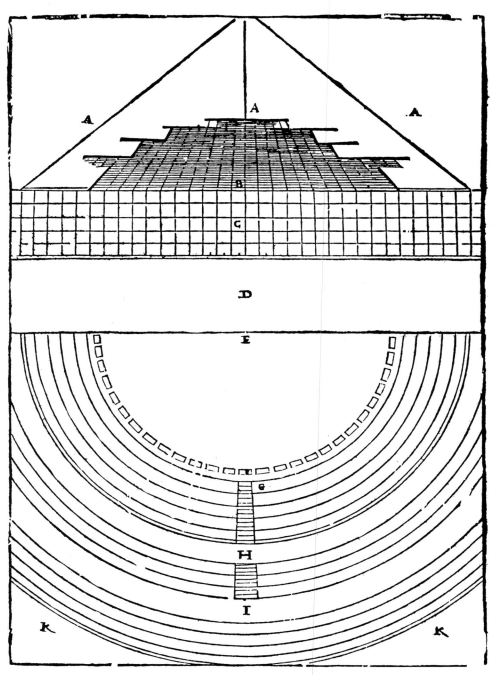

67. Ground plan of Serlio's hall theatre. From *The Second Book of Architecture* (1545).

68. The ducal loggia at Sabbioneta, built 1590. Courtesy Kurt Forster.

privileged spectator, the prince.[14] At Sabbioneta the duke and his party were both elevated and physically separated from the rest of the public in a loggia at the rear of the auditorium (Fig. 68). Here the traditional stage/audience confrontation spaces were given a new political/social message, architecturally reinforced, as historian Kurt Forster notes:

> In simple terms, the stage signified "city square," the ducal loggia indicated "urban palace." They were held in balance, but reality was on the side of the princely spectator, who stood among real columns against a representation of Roman emperors, while the fake architecture of the

[14]Robert Klein and Henri Zerner,"Vitruve et le théâtre de la Renaissance italienne," *Le lieu théâtrale à la renaissance*, ed. Jean Jacquot (Paris, 1964), 54.

Interior Space　**139**

stage was entirely conditioned in its perspective dislocation by the princely point of view.[15]

The spectators in the main part of the hall thus inhabited a somewhat ambiguous symbolic space, its significance entirely derived, as was that of the whole theatre, from the ducal perspective. On the one hand the spectators were a part of the duke's vision, the foreground to the city view that stretched out before his loggia in visual echo of the view of the real city square from the real loggia of his real palace; on the other hand the spectators were less privileged sharers of the ducal vision of the city itself, who had imaginatively to correct their distorted view of that city by calculating their spatial (and thus social) distance from the duke's perfect view.

Sabbioneta's raised loggia did not prove a feature attractive to subsequent theatre designers, but the concept of a raised special space for the sponsoring prince became the central organizing element for most major European theatre auditoriums for the next two centuries. In many of them, perhaps most notably in Richelieu's private theatre in Paris, the prince's space became almost literally the center of the audience space. Here on a raised dais surrounded by other audience members, he became a focus of attention rivaling or surpassing the stage itself.[16] Those unaware of this double focus are often surprised to learn that the auditoriums of Renaissance and baroque theatres were as a rule better illuminated than the stages, and that some of the most desirable seating had a very poor view of the stage and a good view of the auditorium, but these arrangements accurately reflect the importance of these various areas as spaces of public display.

The placing of the actors behind a proscenium arch (an innovation of this style of theatre structure, Richelieu's theatre was the first in France with such a feature) also contributed to privileging the prince's space. This was true not only because of the effects of perspective design already noted, but because the proscenium arch removed the performers from the intimacy and physical dimensionality given them by earlier thrust stages, a loss correspondingly offset by the prince, who could be observed in his full dimensionality on his central dais.

Following the Renaissance, this central dais generally gave way to another privileged space at the rear of the auditorium, the royal box, a

[15]Kurt Forster, "Stagecraft and Statecraft: The Architectural Integration of Public Life and Theatrical Spectacle in Scamozzi's Theatre at Sabbioneta," *Oppositions* 9 (Summer 1977), 81.
[16]Timothy Murray, "Richelieu's Theatre: The Mirror of a Prince," *Renaissance Drama* 8 (1977), 282.

69. The Ducal Opera in Dresden, 1667, showing a raised dais for the ducal family. Otto Weddigen, *Geschichte der Theater Deutschlands* (1904).

space closely related to the loggia at Sabbioneta. The first royal box (with direct access, as at Sabbioneta, from the palace) was built at the Grosses Opernhaus in Dresden in 1664, although a throne in the parterre continued to be used there for great occasions (Fig. 69). Here the prince lost his dimensionality but retained his visual control of the scenic perspective and was able to present a frontal view of his person to his subjects. Moreover, the box allowed a far greater amount of symbolic decoration, reinforcing the glories of the individual within. This box of course remained symbolically even when not literally the center of the auditorium space. Rarely did the royal box stand alone, as did the Sabbioneta loggia; most were in the center of ranks of other, naturally less impressive boxes, for other prominent members of society (Fig. 70).

70. The Zwinger theatre, Dresden, 1746, with royal box at the right. Courtesy Österreichische Nationalbibliothek.

The idea of dividing open galleries into boxes for the aristocracy is attributed to Benedetto Ferrari, who designed the Teatro San Cassiano in Venice in 1637.[17] During the following century rows of boxes lining the auditorium walls became standard in European theatres, and this architectural feature remained common until well into the twentieth century. Its longevity was clearly due not to its usefulness for viewing the spectacle, for which such boxes are generally unsatisfactory, but for its importance in clarifying the social semiotics of the auditorium. Pierre Patte in the most widely read essay on theatre architecture in the late eighteenth century, acknowledged the superiority, in terms of sight lines, of the seating in the classical amphitheatre, but called such seating "too contrary to our customs and manners. We have become accustomed to boxes; they allow everyone to attend the theatre according to his rank and means and to gather there with his usual social companions."[18] The possession of a box, especially of a box at the opera, came to be regarded as one of the more dependable signs of membership in the privileged classes, so much so that even in the

[17]A. E. Brinckmann, *Die Baukunst des 17. und 18. Jahrhunderts in den romanischen Ländern* (Berlin, 1919), 147.
[18]Pierre Patte, *Essai sur l'architecture théâtrale* (Paris, 1782), 165.

democratic United States, the Metropolitan Opera was originally built not primarily to satisfy a public desire for this art, but because all the "aristocratic" boxes at the old Academy of Music were filled by immovable members of the established rich, the Cuttings, the Schuylers, the Van Rensselaers. Rather than settle for symbolically inferior space, the new money represented by the Vanderbilts, the Astors, and the Morgans felt obliged to build its own opera house (Fig. 71).[19]

As the most powerful element symbolically in the public area of the theatre, the boxes have received more attention and elaboration historically than any other spatial element. Often not only the prince but many other box holders were considered the permanent owners of these spaces; the boxes were essentially extensions of their private dwellings. Of course in the ducal theatres erected within private palaces this was literally true, and even in certain detached theatres, such as that at Sabbioneta and the baroque Burgtheater in Vienna, the princely box was connected with the prince's private apartments in the neighboring palace by an enclosed elevated walkway, similar to that which still connects the Palazzo Vecchio and the Palazzo Pitti in Florence. In Renaissance Spain, certain families held the same boxes for generations, passing them on in their wills with other property, and in some cases these too were connected by passageways to adjoining aristocratic houses so that a literal extension of the private dwelling reached into the public playhouse.[20]

Even an independent box might have several adjacent rooms that converted it into a small private suite, furnished with the owner's personal belongings (Fig. 72). A private sitting room often extended behind the actual box, and in Italian opera houses of the later eighteenth century there was usually a supplementary dressing room across the internal passageway from the box where servants could prepare food, drink, and ices for the patrons watching the play or socializing in the box itself.[21] When the Drury Lane of 1794 was built on grounds belonging to the duke of Bedford, the duke insisted on a private box (which still exists) not under the control of the theatre, for himself and his heirs, with the Bedford arms on its face, and with its own private entrance and retiring room.[22]

Although the box holders as a group shared the acknowledged superior space in traditional theatres, this space in turn was subdivided into

[19]Quaintance Eaton, *The Miracle of the Met* (New York, 1968), 2.
[20]Hugo Rennert, *The Spanish Stage in the Time of Lope de Vega* (New York, 1963), 53.
[21]John Rosselli, *The Opera Industry in Italy from Cimarosa to Verdi* (Cambridge, 1984), 10.
[22]W. J. Macqueen Pope, *Theatre Royal, Drury Lane* (London, 1945), 214.

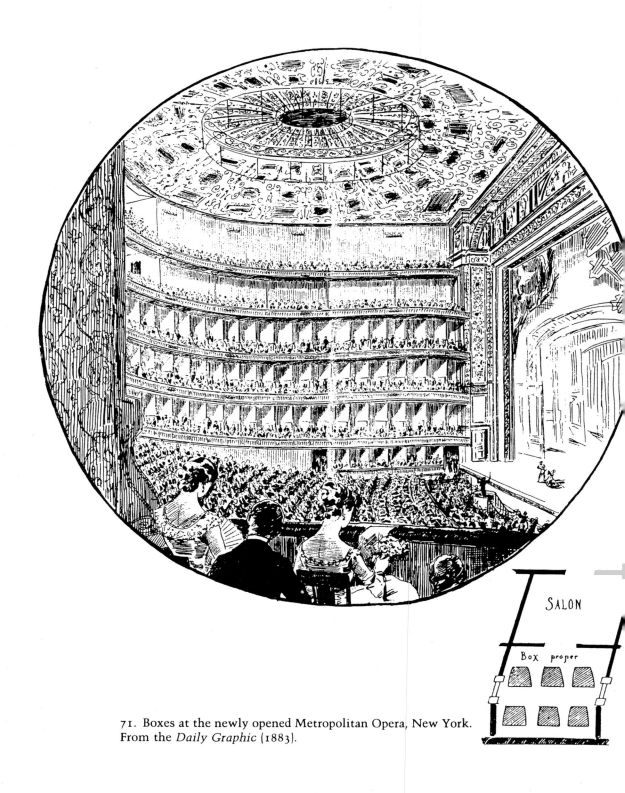

SALON

Box proper

71. Boxes at the newly opened Metropolitan Opera, New York.
From the *Daily Graphic* (1883).

144　　*Places of Performance*

72. Anteroom to the royal box, State Theatre, Prague. Edwin O. Sachs and Ernest A. Woodrow, *Modern Opera Houses and Theatres*, 3 vols. (1896–98).

a highly conscious hierarchy. The second tier of boxes, with the royal box at the center, was always the most prestigious and in many theatres was exclusively the domain of the nobility, moving out in descending order of importance from the royal box as they might be arranged at table for a state dinner. In large theatres in major cities, the first tier was of almost equal standing with the second. Indeed in Vienna boxes in the first and second ranks of the Hofburg and Kärntnertor theatres were limited by law to members of the high aristocracy,[23] and although the law was repealed in 1848, no ordinary burgher, even by 1900, would have thought of occupying one of them.[24]

In some theatres the third tier was of almost equal standing with the

[23]Hannes Stekl, *Österreichs Aristokratie im Vormärz* (Vienna, 1973), 146–47.
[24]Otto Friedländer, *Letzter Glanz der Märchenstadt: Das war Wien um 1900* (Vienna, 1976), 136.

first and second, but normally its rank was distinctly lower, and there the nobility might be mixed with such professionals as lawyers, doctors, and civil servants. One of the democratic reforms instituted by the French when they gained control of Turin during the Napoleonic era was to allow the bourgeoisie access to all three tiers, and when the king was restored he aroused serious protest by insisting upon a return to the traditional restriction of boxes to aristocrats.[25] Higher tiers, if any, were of lower status still, but so long as they remained divided into boxes, as they were in many Italian opera houses until well into the nineteenth century, they might still shelter impoverished members of the aristocracy along with the bourgeoisie.

The removing of the partitions and the converting of this upper area into a gallery in the French or English style were invariable signs that the theatre was seeking a more democratic audience, perhaps even that it was considering giving up the performance of opera altogether (Fig. 73). George Saunders in his 1790 *Treatise on Theatres* considered that whether boxes or galleries were present to be an essential difference between opera houses and "common theatres," since the latter require "accommodations for every class of people, but the former more particularly for those of the first rank, and so disposed that they who choose may be divided into separate companies."[26] In Italy especially, the change to galleries was resisted. The Fenice theatre in Venice did not possess a gallery until 1878, and as late as 1880 the new Teatro Costanzi suffered a near boycott from Rome's aristocrats because its two galleries and only three tiers of boxes branded it as a "popular" theatre.[27] Some Italian public theatres were protected from incursions because they were owned by boxholders' associations, which paid extremely close attention to maintaining social distinctions within the theatre space. The executive body managing one of the Lucca theatres in the early nineteenth century was made up of eight men, two elected from each of the four tiers, and meetings were invalid unless each tier was represented.[28]

One other type of box enjoyed particular social distinction, especially during the eighteenth century: the box located at the side of the stage, within the proscenium arch on the continent, beside the extended forestage in England. The custom of seating certain privileged spectators on the stage seems to have begun in the early seventeenth century. No seating in the theatre provided a less satisfactory view of a

[25]Mme de Boigne, *Mémoires*, ed. J. C. Berchet, 2 vols. (Paris, n.d.), 1:291.
[26]George Saunders, *A Treatise on Theatres* (London, 1790), 33.
[27]V. Frajese, *Dal costanzi all'opera*, 2 vols. (Rome, 1978), 1:45.
[28]Rosselli, *Opera Industry*, 39–45.

73. Auditorium of Drury Lane in London about 1790. From Robert Wilkinson, *Londina Illustrata* (1825).

perspective setting, or of the actors, who tended to work essentially in a downstage line near the footlights, but the occupants of this space shared with the actors the regards of the rest of the audience and indeed even of the inhabitant of the royal box. In France, these visually prominent boxes were in fact appropriated in the seventeenth century for royalty, the king and his attendants on one side of the stage, the queen and her attendants on the other. The disappearance of the king from the French political system was followed almost immediately by the disappearance of his traditional theatrical space. The new Théâtre National (subsequently the Opéra), opened only six months after the trial and execution of Louis XVI, was the first major theatre in France to drop the customary forestage boxes, though they remained in use in England and elsewhere (Fig. 74).

The removal of the royal boxes was quite inadequate for the French

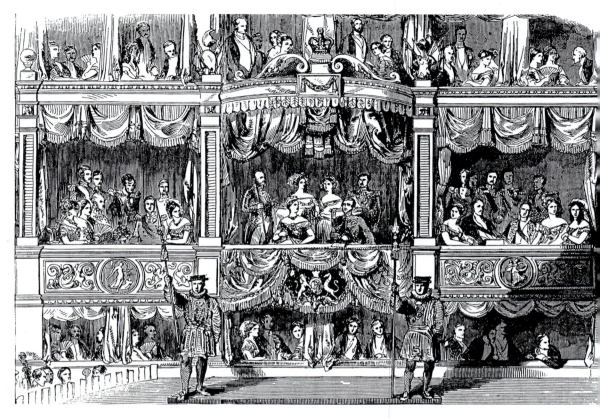

74. Royal box (center) at side of stage in Her Majesty's, London, in 1847. Victor Glasstone Theatre Architecture Collection.

National Convention's Committee on Public Instruction, now placed in control of French theatre. In a decree of March 1794, the committee condemned the entire traditional system of box seating as aristocratic. The closed Comédie Française was totally remodeled that spring to become the first major theatre in Europe since ancient times to contain no boxes or balconies, only a single huge sweep of seats from the pit to the ceiling.[29] This radical innovation in turn lasted scarcely longer than the political reorganization that inspired it. The Directory, which came to power in late 1795, ordered another remodeling the following summer which essentially restored the Comédie to its prerevolutionary state, and Napoleon completed the architectural reaction in 1807

[29]Paul d'Estrée, *Le théâtre sous la terreur* (Paris, 1913), 31–32.

by making it an imperial theatre with an ornate imperial box in the traditional continental style in the center of the auditorium.[30]

Although theatres have traditionally made their most obvious social statements in the specific seating arrangements, these statements are almost invariably reinforced and elaborated by other spatial arrangements in the public areas of the playhouse. This process is already clearly operative even in the early and relatively simple theatre at Sabbioneta (Fig. 75). Social distinctions in the audience are signaled not only in the seating, but in every public space within the theatre, beginning with access to the building. The ducal party entered, as we have observed, by a private walkway, not even requiring that they venture outside. The gentiluomini and gentildonne entered through a portal on the north end, the same end as the ducal loggia, and each had their own foyer, the men on the ground floor, the women upstairs behind the loggia. A doorway led from the men's foyer directly into the seated tiers reserved for the aristocracy at the rear of the auditorium. The general public was provided with no foyer; they entered directly into their seating area in the orchestra through a portal in the middle of the long west side of the building.[31]

Here in embryo was the most common spatial arrangement for European theatres through the eighteenth century. The prince in his loggia (later the central royal box), the lesser aristocracy seated near the prince in slightly less favorable locations, and the general public standing or seated in the orchestra or pit below. Later, when a more distinct class of merchants, clerks, and professional men developed, especially in England, these claimed the pit as their territory, while footmen, grooms, and other such marginal members of society were relegated to rows of benches in the remote and uncomfortable area above the boxes, the galleries or paradise.

Very frequently these divisions were so arranged that although all spectators shared the same auditorium, there was little or no actual overlapping of social spaces. Once again, the Sabbioneta theatre contained the germ of such divisions. During the baroque period private access to the central box was the most common separation of non-auditorium space, but as a more heterogeneous public began to attend the major theatres of Europe, the social ambiguity of such public spaces as lobbies and foyers began to cause concern in some quarters. When redesigning London's Drury Lane in 1813, Benjamin Wyatt re-

[30]L. H. Lecomte, *Napoléon et le monde dramatique* (Paris, 1912), 108.
[31]Forster, "Stagecraft," 66.

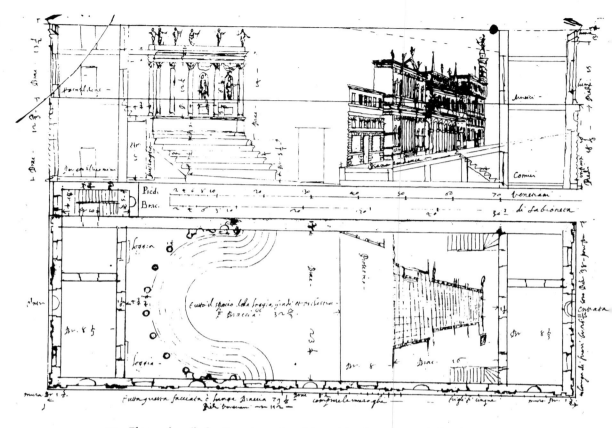

75. Floor plan (below) and section (above) by Scamozzi of the theatre at Sabbioneta. A walkway (not shown) gave access to the loggia from the east (top of the plan). The entrance for the nobility is at the center of the left wall on this plan, and section has "gentiluomini" and "gentildonne" written in the appropriate spaces at the same left end. The horseshoe-shaped seating in the center of the plan was for the nobility, with the ducal loggia behind it (to the left). The public entrance was through the center of the long bottom wall on the plan (indicated by a rectangular element in the center of the section). The stage, with dimensional perspective scenery, as at Vicenza, occupies the right half of both drawings.

marked that among the various reforms need in London theatres none seemed more important than that of "protecting the more rational and respectable class of spectators from those nuisances to which they have long been exposed" by passing through "lobbies, rooms, and avenues crowded with the most disreputable members of the commonity, and subject to scenes of the most disgusting indecency." Wyatt's solution to this problem was to remove all lobbies, coffee rooms, and lounges from the dress circle area and to provide a "spacious and hand-some suite of rooms" on the next floor "for the purpose of attracting all those whom it is desireable to remove from below the stairs and keeping them out of the way of the more respectable part of the company."[32]

This solution, providing larger and more attractive public spaces for the less privileged members of the audience, was of course totally at odds with conventional social semiotics of space, and most subsequent London theatres approached the problem in a more direct if more coercive manner, by providing separate entrances for those seated in separate areas of the theatre (Fig. 76) and suiting the connecting interior spaces to the elegance of the public destined for each part of the auditorium. Thus the patrons of the dress circle, first boxes, or stalls approached through the largest and most lavishly decorated lobbies and stairway, whereas patrons of the upper gallery were given only the minimum modest stairs and passageways to reach their humble places. The 1871 lobby arrangement of the Royal Victoria Palace Theatre in London (originally the Royal Coburg and later known as the Old Vic) provides a clear and fairly typical example of how such divisions were managed, even in a rather small total space and in a theatre that did not rely on a wide range of society for support (Fig. 77). The large central entrance led to a lobby and grand stone staircase dominating the available space and serving the patrons of the boxes. On either side of this lobby were retiring and cloak rooms and toilet facilities, one for men, the other for women. At either side of this central space other exterior doors gave access to two much more modest lobbies, leading to the pit. Female pit patrons had access to the retiring room and toilets used also by box patrons, but the equivalent male rooms were accessible to box patrons only. Gallery patrons entered the theatre from an even more modest side door opening directly upon a narrow and winding wooden staircase, without even a pretense of a lobby. When bars or similar refreshment areas, existed, these also varied in size, ornamentation, and comfort according to which area they served.

The great monumental theatres of the eighteenth and nineteenth centuries, especially those devoted to the performance of opera, gave comparatively little attention to such spatial segregation, partly because they were oriented toward a more homogeneous audience from the outset, and partly because as such theatres became the favored gathering places of the new monied classes their public spaces became

[32]Quoted in Woodrow, "Theatres," *Building News and Engineering Journal,* August 24, 1894, 244–45.

76. An 1826 engraving of the Royal Coburg Theatre, London (later the Royal Victoria and eventually the Old Vic). The separate entrances for box, pit, and gallery patrons are clearly marked. Courtesy the Old Vic.

a kind of indoor parade ground not only for the gathering of fashionable society, but even more important, for its display. Audience support spaces proliferated—lobbies, galleries, vestibules, grand staircases, until they occupied, in the great opera houses of the late nineteenth century, more space than either the auditorium or the stage (Fig. 78). Less wealthy patrons were not excluded from such spaces provided they could afford to attend the opera at all, but like the lesser audience members in a ducal theatre of the Renaissance: they were welcome as spectators, not of the opera itself, but of the magnificence of those members of society who could be seen there and who displayed them-

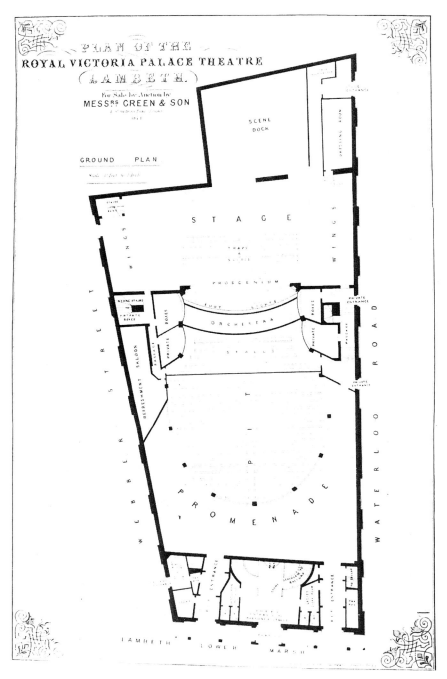

77. Floor plan of the Royal Victoria Palace Theatre, London, in 1871.
Courtesy the Old Vic.

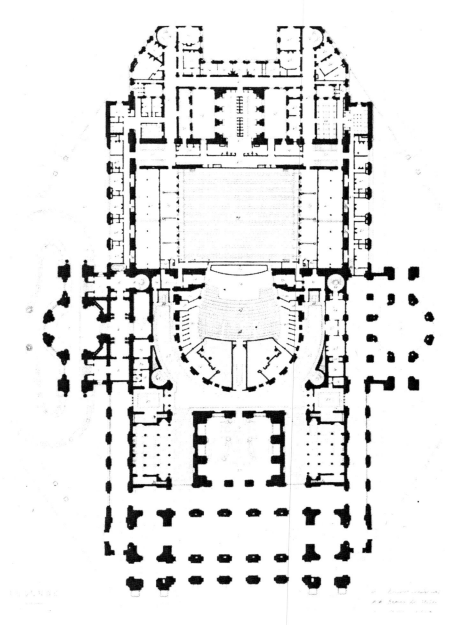

78. Floor plan of the Paris Opéra. Edwin O. Sachs and Ernest A. Woodrow, *Modern Opera Houses and Theatres*, 3 vols. (1896–98).

selves in the great foyers and on the grand staircases at intermissions (Fig. 79).

The continental casualness on this point was a matter of some concern to English theorists, as may be seen in an article in *Building News*

79. The grand staircase of the Paris Opéra. Courtesy Bibliothèque Nationale, Opéra.

of 1862 which notes: "There is scarcely a theatre in London the approaches to which are not superior to those of the theatres in Paris, for here the visitor to pit, boxes, and galleries are separated, whereas across the channel the same doorway serves for all, in most cases, and even, in the French Theatre, the visitors to boxes and galleries descend the same staircases."[33]

This comment was subsequently cited by a French architectural theorist as evidence that despite the highly socially stratified seating in continental theatres, French theatre architecture was more truly democratic than English: "A theatre belongs to everyone, and every spectator must be able to move about as he would in his own home."[34]

Except in the design of opera houses, themselves rather exotic structures there, theatres in England were in fact somewhat more democratic in seating arrangements than most continental theatres. They traditionally did not follow the standard continental model of rows of boxes surrounding a central pit, but placed at the rear of the auditorium one or more great sweeping galleries, a type of seating much more congenial to a middle-class audience. Rows of boxes remained common on the sides of the auditorium, but these became increasingly vestigial in the late nineteenth and early twentieth centuries as the function of the theatre as a place of social display faded. The privacy of the box still possessed a distinct social value, but for patrons interested in seeing the play, the gallery and pit were distinctly preferable locations. To respond to this concern, theatre managers began to divide the pit, placing more comfortable and more expensive seats in the front part, now renamed the stalls, and separating this more privileged section from the remaining pit by a physical barrier. The number of stalls a theatre possessed became a clear expression of its expectations about the social class of its audience, as an architect explained near the close of the nineteenth century: "The size of the stalls and the number of rows depend upon the class of house: in the East-End and provinces two or three rows are sufficient, while in the West-End of London there are cases where the whole level of this area is occupied with stalls."[35]

As the aristocratic public, whose domain the boxes traditionally had been, became a less significant element in the theatre audience, the Wagnerian auditorium with its democratic seating provided an attractive alternate spatial model (Fig. 80). Today in most theatres where

[33]*Building News and Architectural Journal* 9 (1862), 308.
[34]G. Davioud, *Revue générale de l'architecture* 23 (1865), 123.
[35]Woodrow, "Theatres," *Building News and Engineering Journal*, September 16, 1892, 382.

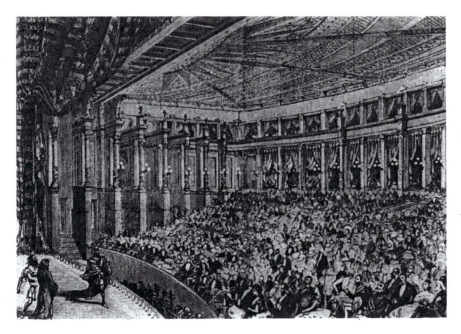

80. The auditorium at Bayreuth. From *Le Théâtre* (1899).

boxes remain, they serve a largely decorative function, adding to the elaboration of the area around the proscenium arch. They may occasionally be used by royalty or other honored guests in echo of their former glory, or even on occasion be filled with actors in costume, as a conscious anachronism to give a period flavor to the revival of a classic play, but most often today these vestigial spaces serve to connote a vague period elegance rather than as potential seating. If they have any utilitarian function, it is often to provide a convenient area for setting up auxiliary lighting equipment.

Economic as well as social forces doomed the theatre wall lined with boxes so typical of the baroque period. As theatres increasingly sought larger audiences, and at the same time sought to accommodate them in as efficient a manner as possible, the great open sweeping balconies of the English theatre proved much more useful than continental boxes. During the late nineteenth and early twentieth centuries the box, pit, and gallery arrangement almost universally gave way to an arrangement of stalls with one or more balconies above. Audiences were still to some extent socially segregated in seating, owing to the differential in seating prices, but the social segregation of other internal spaces, so common in earlier times, generally disappeared under the combined influences of democratic idealism, new fire codes, and economic pressures.

The 1983 remodeling of London's Old Vic provides an excellent case study of the results of changes in the organization of public spaces within European theatres during the last century. Although the official booklet describing the remodeling, *The Old Vic Refurbished*, speaks of the restoring of the theatre to "its former Victorian splendor," interior spatial expectations have so altered that the 1871 configuration with separate entrances and stairways for each social class would have been totally unacceptable for modern use. Now, as in most modern theatres, members of the audience, wherever they are sitting, all enter the theatre through a large central lobby. Those to be seated in the pit pass directly into it through passages at the rear of the lobby, while those to be seated in the two balconies ascend a large staircase at one side of the lobby (Fig. 81). This new staircase, the booklet states proudly, provides "access to all parts of the house," and "replaces the dismal labyrinth an audience was expected to negotiate" during the nineteenth century.[36] Such a comment provides striking testimony of a changed spatial code. Quite likely a modern audience would indeed find the 1871 arrangements a dismal labyrinth, but to the Victorian audiences the various carefully separated entrances, access routes, and public spaces provided, on the contrary, a comforting affirmation of social position and a stable social order.

There is still of course a certain amount of natural separation among public areas in those theatres, common in Europe, which like the Vic offer intermission refreshment and circulation areas on each floor. The most common pattern today is to locate an elegant central lobby inside the main entrance, containing a ticket window but not a bar, and to place the largest and most elegant bar on the first level above this (normally called the dress circle in England). Higher balconies normally all have their own public areas for circulation at intermission and attendant bars, but the space and the bar will become smaller and more modest at each ascending level. Patrons from the highest balcony are now free, as they were not in traditional nineteenth-century theatres, to descend to the more elegant public areas below, but because they must go up and down several flights of stairs to do so, each seating area in fact normally tends to patronize its own circulation area during intermission in a traditional manner. The Palace of Congresses in Moscow offers an impressive socialist alternative to this class distinc-

[36]D. F. Cheshire, Sean McCarthy, and Hilary Norris, *The Old Vic Refurbished* (London, 1983), 36–37.

81. The present lobby of the Old Vic, London. Courtesy the Old Vic.

Up to top of 2nd Gade

tion based on willingness to climb stairs; it sends its entire audience on banks of escalators to the top floor at intermissions during which refreshments are spread out on tables ringing a vast common hall.

New York's Broadway theatres rarely provide even the modest but varied public spaces of most European facade theatres. A small, functional but featureless lobby with a ticket window at one side is often the essential public space, the only common spaces within being whatever stairs are essential and the aisles, rather larger at the rear, where a small bar may sometimes be placed. We are here almost at the opposite extreme from the great European opera houses with their foyers and galleries for interior strolling between the acts. Most Broadway houses are so limited in public spaces aside from the auditorium itself that at intermissions the street in front of the theatre is appropriated as an extension of the main lobby, and a large crowd totally filling the sidewalk before the theatre during intermissions is a common sight during the evenings in this area (Fig. 82). A recent commentator on urban spaces has seen this appropriation as an integral part of the design of such theatres, a "modern form of urban-entertainment architecture," the purpose of which is "to build lavishly, colorfully, and gaudily everywhere, inside and out, as a way of extending the atmosphere of the drama beyond the stage—of bringing it through the auditorium, into

much more similar!

82. A New York theatre audience at intermission. Courtesy the Theatre Collection of the Museum of the City of New York.

83. The State Opera in Hamburg, 1955. From Roberto Aloi, *Architteture per lo spettacolo* (1958), courtesy Ulrico Hoepli.

the lobby, and out onto the street"; the effect is "to surround both audiences and passersby with a festive glow."[37] Although the designers of these theatres were certainly aware of the ambiance of the entire district within which their structures were located, it seems likely that this integration of stage and street space has come about more directly because of the high price of any space in the area of Times Square than because of a thoughtful analysis of urban psychology. Nevertheless, the result unquestionably contributes to the particular ambience and excitement of these theatres.

Designers of modern monumental theatres have often sought to gain something of this same relationship to the city spaces outside. Usually built in locations with less commercial competition for space and normally sheltered in any case at least to some extent from such concerns by public funding, these theatres are traditionally lavish in their use of public space. The same inspiration that creates the parks, verandas, and loggias which often surround them on the outside leads, in interior

[37]Tony Hiss, "Reflections," *The New Yorker*, June 29, 1987, 75.

space, to vast open lobbies and stairways and a general impression of spatial plenitude. Such areas seem conceived not to provide a lavish setting for the display of the attending patrons in the manner of the Paris Opéra, but rather to ==bear witness to the civic spirit== shown by the city or the nation in erecting so formidable a housing for the arts. Even so, the designers of such structures often seem concerned that their monuments will seem too closed off from their surroundings. Therefore these buildings are often opened, at least visually, to the city outside by huge glass walls (Fig. 83). If urban space and theatre space do not truly mix, as they do in the Broadway intermissions, they are at least made ==mutually accessible in visual terms==, and the city population is encouraged to see them as such. In his program for the Malmø City Theatre in Sweden, one of the first theatres with a ==glass facade==, the consultant Per Lindberg insisted that "the foyer must be so open, so gleaming with light that anyone who's thinking of giving the theatre the go-by will think twice and find himself drawn into it."[38]

[38]Quoted in Henrik Sjögren, *Stage and Society in Sweden* (Uddevalla, 1979), 19.

Iron Gate
is disguised
b/c of its
dual function

6.

Interior Decoration

E ven if one regards the theatre building in strictly functional
terms, as a structure for bringing together an audience and a
performance, one can still acknowledge an important practical
function for exterior decoration and ornamentation. Such elements
can serve to identify the building and its purpose and attract its potential public. Once the public has arrived, and particularly after it is
seated, the performance itself might reasonably be expected to provide
all the signification necessary for the theatrical experience. Certainly
it is because they have held this position that many modern theorists
and practitioners have designed auditoriums as physically neutral as
possible and darkened them to focus all attention on the stage, at least
during the actual performance. For much of the history of the theatre,
however, interior decoration has been one of the building's richest
sources of signification. The reason for this apparent contradiction is,
as we have seen in our examination of internal and external spatial
configurations, that the physical theatre has rarely if ever been solely a
space for the confrontation of audience and performance. It has almost
always served a great variety of other social and cultural functions, all
of which have added to the complexity of both its external and its
internal signifying systems.

In the court theatres of the Renaissance and the baroque period,
erected, as we have seen, less for artistic ends than for the display of
princely wealth and power, the internal decorations naturally echoed
the richness of the surrounding palace. Indeed, the theatre, as a center
of display and of pleasure, was often one of the most elaborately decorated parts of a princely dwelling. The earliest public commercial theatres in Italy, though unable to equal such ostentation, nonetheless

attempted to attract a public by offering not simply performances but also the opportunity to spend a few hours in elegant surroundings. Theatre has traditionally presented itself as a special experience set apart from everyday life, an experience not restricted to the actual performance but extending to the entire event structure of which the performance is a part, and the location of that event structure has often carried forward that image by displaying the symbols of elegance, pleasure, and high culture.

Like internal spatial arrangements, interior decoration in the early theatres of the Italian Renaissance was selected to emphasize the importance and magnificence of the sponsors. Costly and elegant decorative materials naturally contributed to this end, but even more important was the decorative vocabulary governing the use of these materials. The primary source for symbols of power and authority at this time was classical, especially Roman, antiquity; Rome replaced Jerusalem as the symbolic model for all cities. The very idea of building permanent theatre structures arose from a desire to recapture classical pomp and display, and the first theatres drew most of their inspiration from the study of ancient ruins and from the architectural manuals of Vitruvius. A central work of reference for Renaissance theatre architects was Sebastiano Serlio's book on architecture, the third volume of which contained his material on the building of Roman theatres. One of Serlio's frontispieces shows the ruins of a rusticated Roman arch, above it the legend *Roma Quanta Fuit Ipsa Ruina Docet* "the grandeur of Rome is demonstrated by its ruins" (Fig. 84). By building imitations of these ruins, the Renaissance princes hoped to create signs that would evoke a similar grandeur.

This symbolic importance of Renaissance theatres is really less clear in the specific physical arrangements copied (on a reduced scale) from Roman models than in their decorative elements, which rarely reproduced the specific decorative devices of Roman theatres but rather were intended to evoke images of classical grandeur in the minds of a Renaissance audience. The decoration of the earliest permanent theatres of the Renaissance intertwine references to their contemporary sponsors with Roman motifs.

Thus the Teatro Olimpico in Vicenza, sponsored by a learned Academy, honored no single prince in its internal decoration, but celebrated its own organization and membership visually in classical terms. The most prominent visual element in the interior is the huge permanent scenic facade designed by Palladio (Fig. 85). Its most striking element is the ninety-five statues it contains, most of them supported and framed by classical architectural elements and recalling the gods, heroes, and

QVINTO LIBRO D'ARCHITETTVRA,
DI SEBASTIAN SERLIO BOLOSGNESE,
Nel quale si tratta di diuerse forme di Tempij sacri, secondo il co-
stume Christiano, & al modo antico.
Aggiuntoui le misure che seruono a tutti li ordini de cōponimēti, che vi si cōtēgono.

ROMA QVANTA FVIT IPSA RVINA DOCET

84. Frontispiece to Book 5 of Serlio's *Architettura*, 1545.

85. Interior of the Teatro Olimpico at Vicenza. *Theatre Arts,* 1921.

emperors found on the similarly elaborate permanent stage facades of theatres of the Roman Empire. At Vicenza, however, these statues are of local dignitaries and members of the Academy. The Academy is further celebrated and related to Roman grandeur by the decoration over the monumental central opening in the scenic facade. There appears the seal of the Academy with its motto *Hoc Opus* and a representation of a Roman theatre constructed for the public games. Below these are placed the coat of arms of the city of Vicenza and a monumental inscription in Latin hailing the genius of the Academy as expressed in the erection of the theatre. The intellectual feats of the Academy were symbolically tied to the physical feats of Hercules, to whom the building was dedicated and whose exploits were celebrated on a series of large bas-reliefs running around the upper area of the

86. Exterior of the theatre
at Sabbioneta. Courtesy
Kurt Forster.

facade and out into the theatre above the main entrances, next to the
stage on either side.[1]

The theatre at Sabbioneta was even more specific and programmatic
in its Roman decorative citation. Its exterior doors were almost exact
copies of the Serlio frontispiece with rusticated frames and *Roma
Quanta Fuit . . .* repeated on a band running around the building above
the rusticated doors and windows (Fig. 86). Entering this theatre
through its main door, audience members first observed on the opposite wall a fresco of a Roman arch bearing a variant of the motto
inscribed on the exterior. Within this arch appeared a painted view of
the Capitoline Hill in Rome. Once within the theatre, the spectator
could turn to find an echoing trompe d'oeil fresco, which frames the
entrance and depicts another triumphal arch honoring the then emperor Rudolf II and framing another Roman view, that of the tomb of
the emperor Hadrian (Fig. 87).

[1]Antonio Magrini, *Il teatro olimpico nuovamente descritto ed illustrato* (Padua:
1847).

87. Interior side wall of Sabbioneta theatre with view of the Castel Sant'Angelo. Courtesy Kurt Forster.

Art historian Kurt Forster has noted that these iconic *vedute* (views), besides relating symbolically to the power and grandeur of Rome as city and empire, serve indexically to refer to a whole system of interlocking spatial and ideological relationships. The city-ruler, east-west axis represented by the two frescos is echoed in the city-ruler north-south axis formed by the prince's loggia and the stage. Moreover the frescos tie the real Sabbioneta's topography to that of classical (and mythic) Rome; the town square of Sabbioneta lies behind the Capitoline fresco and the Gonzaga fortress and palace behind that of the Castel Saint'Angelo. Sixteenth-century maps of ancient Rome placed the Roman theatre district and the great circuses of Agonalis and Flaminius (represented on the Olimpico seal) between the

Capitoline and Hadrian's tomb, so the frescos not only suggested parallels between the urban design of Sabbioneta and that of classical Rome, but placed the theatre itself in an echoing central position (Fig. 88).[2]

At both Vicenza and Sabbioneta the theatres contained a loggia composed of Roman columns, topped with heroic figures, and with inset niches holding imperial busts, but the center of the loggia was closed at the democratic Olimpico in Vicenza and open at Sabbioneta so that the prince could appear there surrounded by architectual and sculptural signs of imperial glory (Fig. 68). In later theatres, this decorative cluster was to be repeated in the similarly placed royal box.

The Farnese theatre at Parma, opened in 1619, already showed the beginnings of a somewhat different decorative vocabulary, one that would become typical of baroque theatres. Although certain Roman architectural details were utilized, the designers made little effort to recall in the Farnese's decoration the grandeur of classical ruins. The emphasis was more specifically on the recent achievements of its own princely patrons, the Medici and the Farnesi, and its decoration emphasized the theatre's role as a repository of culture in general rather than as the inheritor of a certain architectural tradition.

Thus the grand vestibule offered frescos on the one hand celebrating the military victories of the Medici and Farnese troops, with the heroes feted in Elysian Fields, and on the other hand showing Mount Parnassus, where the great poets Boccaccio, Dante, and Apollo, welcomed the great Medici, Francesco, Giuliano and Cosimo. In the auditorium above the boxes rose pedestals for statues not of imperial heroes but of Apollo and the nine muses. These free-standing figures were an important departure from the decoration at Vicenza and Sabbioneta, where male heroes, patrons, and emperors dominated and female figures appeared only in lesser decorative elements such as arabesques.

Roman triumphal arches, as at Sabbioneta, formed the side entrances to the Farnese theatre, but here these were decorated not with Roman architectural views but with equestrian statues of the Farnese dukes Ottavio and Alessandro (Fig. 89). The most common decorative element, found here in abundance for the first time, was the allegorical figure, which would remain a mainstay of theatrical embellishment for the next several centuries. Around the upper balcony were figures representing Immortality, Fame, Fortune, Heroic Virtue, Vigilance, Goodness, Eloquence, Dignity, and Reason, and around the proscenium

---

[2]Kurt W. Forster, "Stagecraft and Statecraft: The Architectural Integration of Public Life and Theatrical Spectacle in Scamozzi's Theatre at Sabbioneta," *Oppositions* 9 (Summer 1977), 78–85.

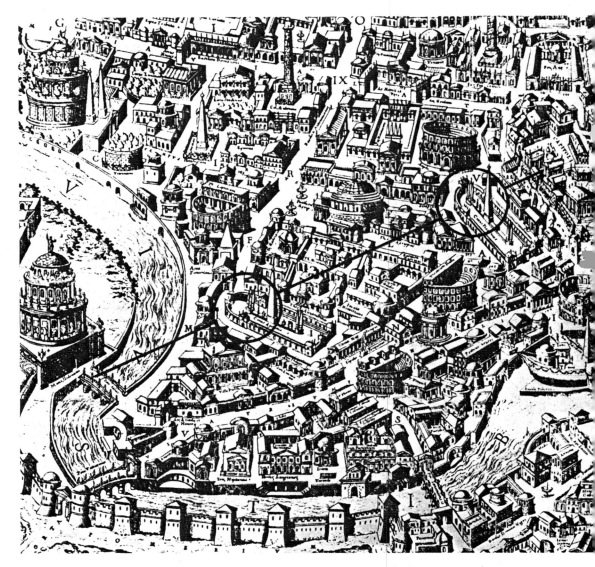

88. Stefano Duperac's view of ancient Rome, published in 1574. A line connecting the Capitoline Hill at the right with Hadrian's tomb passes through the circled Circus Agonalis and the Circus Flaminius. Courtesy Kurt Forster.

opening were Mirth, Sadness, Poetry, Pröse, Magnificence, Good and Bad Fortune, Generosity, and Military Valor, along with the more obviously relevant Tragedy, Comedy, and Dithyramb. The equestrian statues were also supported by allegorical figures—Liberty and Intrepidity for Duke Ottavio and Victory and Military Strategy for Duke

89. Interior of the Farnese theatre, Parma. *Theatre Arts*, 1922.

Alessandro. On the side walls appeared Peace, War, Arms, Honor, Security, Glory, the Golden Age, and the Silver Age.[3]

In sum, the Farnese theatre marks an important new direction in the interior decoration of European theatres, not only in its extensive use of allegorical elements but, equally strikingly, in its departure from the use of specifically classical references as primary authenticating elements and the substitution for them of the cultural, political, and military values of the sponsoring princely family. Thus the spatial appropriation of the baroque theatre by the sponsoring prince was reflected also in the accumulation of decorative symbols honoring the patron.

The auditorium of seventeenth- and eighteenth-century theatres was the most elaborately decorated area of the building, its lavishness especially striking when, as in the German baroque churches of the same period, it was manifested within a rather plain and severe exteri-

[3]Paolo Donati Parmigiano, *Descrizione del gran teatro Farnese di Parma* (Parma, 1817).

or. Details varied greatly from theatre to theatre and from country to country, but the general vocabulary and grammar of ornament were remarkably consistent, partly because of the very similar cultural roles of these structures and partly because many of the most influential of them were designed by members of a few key families, most notably the Bibienas.

These more or less consistent interior arrangements provided a fairly limited number of spaces within the auditorium for decorative display. The side walls, major decorative areas in the theatres at Sabbioneta and Parma, were in later auditoriums covered with ranks of boxes and thus much reduced in visual importance. Accordingly, the decoration of the major axis of the princely theatres, with the royal box at one end and the stage at the other, gained much more focus. The fronts of the side boxes, relatively small areas in any case, were always subordinated to this axis in decoration. The other major area available for decoration was the auditorium ceiling, and baroque theatres, like baroque palaces and public buildings, usually had ceilings rich in decorative elaboration.

The decorations of the royal box were clearly designed to reinforce its position as the psychological center of the auditorium. Often this box was more elaborate than the stage, to which, in fact, it sometimes appeared to be a rival. Thus the castle theatre (1766) at Böhmisch-Krumau has a ducal box within a proscenium arch and theatrical curtains; less obvious theatrical frames such as side columns and overhead draperies are standard features of such boxes (Fig. 90). All the conventional emblems of power and glory were used to enhance the magnificence of these boxes, though the particularly martial references of the Farnese theatre gradually gave way to a more generalized neoclassic decorative vocabulary and motifs celebrating such attributes of the Renaissance prince as valor and virtue to more neutral themes. These depictions included Olympian deities, supporting caryatids and *atlantides*, crowns and eagles, ornamental classic vases, figures with palms, globes, and trumpets, putti bearing floral wreathes, and suitable memorials. The decorative vocabulary of the princely theatres of the baroque era was frequently copied in public theatres, where it was aimed to suggest aristocratic elegance without the specific patronage of the prince. This generally predictable decorative repertoire of wreaths and swags, gods and muses, classic vases and balustrades, draperies and putti, adorned most theatres until nearly the end of the eighteenth century and remained a feature of those seeking a traditional aristocratic ambiance for a century more. Describing a typical example of such display at the 1816 Teatro San Carlo in Naples (Fig. 91),

90. The court theatre of Böhmisch-Krumau, 1766, with its ducal box. Margarete Baur-Heinhold, *Theater des Barock* (1966). Courtesy Verlag Callwey.

Stendhal wrote: "I can conceive of nothing more majestic or more magnificent than the sumptuous Royal Box, which is set astride the central doorway, raised aloft on two great golden palm trees, each of natural size; the hangings are fashioned out of leaves of metal, tinted in the palest red; even the crown, that superannuated emblem, seems scarcely too absurd."[4] Even the emblematic cartouche with a coat of arms or a Latin motto commemorating the erection of the theatre, which in the Vicenza Olimpico and the Farnese held a commanding position over the center of the stage, is in later baroque theatres placed instead over this box, among all the panoply of columns, crowns, eagles, and putti. Typical is the box of the Markgräfliches Opernhaus at Bayreuth, above which a baroque cartouche proclaims "Pro Friederico

[4]Stendhal, *Rome, Florence, et Naples en 1817* (Paris, 1956), 41.

91. Interior of the San Carlo opera (1816), with the royal box. From Roberto Aloi, *Architetture per lo spettacolo* (1958). Courtesy Ulrico Hoepli.

et Sophia Josephus Gallus Bibiena Fecit. Ano Domi MDCCXLVIII" (Fig. 92).

The boxes extending to either side of the royal box were naturally much more modest in decoration, as befitted their subordinate position. Individual boxes were traditionally not given special treatment; this mark was reserved for the sponsoring prince. Either all boxes were treated decoratively in much the same way (as in the first great public opera houses of Venice and in the majority of subsequent public theatres) or each tier was treated as a decorative unit, with the one on the same level as the royal box being the most elaborately decorated. Frequently, as at Bayreuth, this tier had three-dimensional balustrades fronting each box, while more modest tiers had to be content with painted panels.

The box fronts, separated by column bases or other dividing elements, formed a natural rhythmical sequence around the auditorium. Decorators sometimes used a repeated design motif on the front of each box (such as the laurel swags on box fronts of the 1792 Drury Lane in London) or a series of bas-reliefs, friezes, or paintings on a common theme. The 1767 court theatre at Versailles illustrates such a pattern (Fig. 93). The lowest level of boxes is fronted with bas-reliefs of the Olympian gods and their attributes, on panels separated by medallions bearing heads of the muses. The next tier offers bas-reliefs of putti frolicking on clouds and playing musical instruments, on panels separated by carved wreathes surrounding signs of the zodiac. The third tier, on the level of the royal box, is a series of balustrades separated by classical vases in bas-relief.[5] The first stirrings of romanticism introduced other visual elements into this traditional vocabulary. During the 1790s several small Parisian theatres acquired "gothic" interiors, with boxes looking more suitable for cathedral stalls than theatre accommodation. Some other theatres reflected the contemporary political enthusiasm with the installation of simple boxes undecorated except for bands of red, white, and blue, while in still others, already existing baroque columns and putti were painted in the same colors, creating a bizarre, if patriotic, effect. A similarly nationalistic interest determined the decoration of a number of American theatres built shortly after the Revolution. Thus the Walnut Street Theatre in Philadelphia (1809) had box fronts decorated with paintings representing the land and sea battles of that war. The medallions separating these scenes depicted not muses, but patriotic heroes—presidents and founding fathers on the first tier, generals on the second, and naval

[5]André Japy, L'opéra royal de Versailles (Versailles, 1958), 65.

92. Ducal box at the Bayreuth Opera, 1748. Margarete Baur-Heinhold, *Theater des Barock* (1966). Courtesy Verlag Callwey.

93. Interior, Versailles court theatre. Margarete Baur-Heinhold, *Theater des Barock* (1966). Courtesy Verlag Callwey.

heroes on the third.[6] The romantic era also brought a fresh interest in national drama, and representations of national dramatists or scenes from their plays joined or replaced the traditional depictions of classical subjects. The fronts of the boxes at the Paris Variétés (1807) showed scenes featuring the popular characters Margot, Jocrisse, and Cadet-Roussel, all dressed, however, in classical robes to ensure their aesthetic respectability.[7] The dress circle fronts of the Drury Lane theatre of 1812 presented scenes from thirteen of the Shakespearian plays most popular at that period.[8]

The proscenium arch, a standard feature in the European theatre from the early seventeenth century onward, did not attempt to rival the baroque royal box in decorative elaboration. The first such arch, in the Farnese theatre, is unique in the amount, if not in the subject matter, of such decoration (Fig. 94). The niches surrounding its stage opening recall those at Vicenza, but here offer a rich selection of allegorical figures rather than local dignitaries—Magnificence, Good and Evil Fortune, Generosity, and Military Valor, along with the more clearly relevant Mirth, Sadness, Poetry, Prose, Tragedy, Comedy, and Dithyramb. In most subsequent European theatres the major decorative element of the sides of the proscenium was a pair of massive columns, normally with some version of a Corinthian capital. Between them were placed either stage boxes or decorative elements, most commonly life-size statuary on pedestals or in niches. During the French Revolution, large allegorical statues of Liberty and Equality stood in these spots, but more often they were such figures as Comedy and Tragedy or Theatre and Music. Occasionally they represented appropriate figures from the history of the genre, such as Molière and Corneille.

The space at the top center of the proscenium arch, its visual focus architecturally, was the most important location for the placement of symbolic elements. In that space the Vicenza Olimpico displayed the coat of arms of the city, and there the Farnese court also placed its coat of arms on a baroque shield resting on a drapery held by a pair of putti. The pattern thus established was followed throughout the baroque period, with the emblems of the sponsoring prince or city placed in that spot, and some theatres even today preserve this custom. In pre-

[6]F. C. Wemyss, *Twenty-Six Years in the Life of an Actor and Manager* (New York, 1847), 234–35.

[7]Pierre Vaisse, "Le décor peint des salles de spectacle," *Les monuments historiques de la France* 4 (1978), 68.

[8]Edward W. Brayley, *Historical and Descriptive Accounts of the Theatres of London* (London, 1833), 10.

94. The stage of the Farnese theatre, Parma. *Theatre Arts,* 1922.

Revolutionary France, almost every public theatre displayed in this position a shield with the royal fleurs-de-lis, while princely theatres in Italy, Spain, and Germany displayed the appropriate armorial device for their sponsor (Fig. 95). Naturally during the French Revolution other political symbols succeeded those of royalty. The shield with the fleurs-de-lis on the proscenium arch at Versailles was replaced by the coat of arms of the Revolutionary Jacobin Club and the crown atop the shield covered (though not replaced) by a Phrygian cap. The cap was removed after the Revolution and the fleurs-de-lis reappeared under Louis Philippe.[9]

Rarely did these devices stand alone; they were emphasized by the same traditional signs of power and glory (though in more modest size) as those that surrounded the facing royal box—surmounted by crowns,

[9]Japy, *Opéra royal,* 97.

95. Cartouche over center of proscenium, Versailles court theatre. Margarete Baur-Heinhold, *Theater des Barock* (1966). Courtesy Verlag Callwey.

trailing banners or clouds, backed by golden shafts suggesting metallic sunbursts, and usually supported by allegorical figures on either side. These were typically angels, often with trumpets emblematic of fame and glory, on the continent, and the lion and unicorn in England. London's Royal Victoria Theatre (today the Old Vic) backed this traditional emblem in the mid-nineteenth century with four national flags, and the emblem remains today in the auditorium restored in 1983 by a Canadian entrepreneur, though the backing flags are now the Union Jack, the flag of St. George, and those of the city of Toronto and of the Dominion of Canada.[10] The sponsoring princes have disappeared, but their semiotic tradition lives on in this contemporary emblematic display celebrating a Canadian businessman (Fig. 96).

The most extensive area open for decorative display in most theatre auditoriums is the ceiling, and each historical period in Western theatre has tended to favor some particular mode of ceiling treatment. In palaces and government buildings of the Renaissance and the baroque era the ceilings of major rooms were regularly decorated with elaborate murals, frequently depicting gods, classical heroes, and allegorical figures amid clouds, classical temples, and expanses of sky. The knowledge that theatres in antiquity had in fact been open to the heavens encouraged this tradition. Indeed some Renaissance theatres were given ceilings that simply depicted an open sky or, on occasion, a

[10]D. F. Cheshire, Sean McCarthy, and Hilary Norris, *The Old Vic Refurbished* (London, 1983), 16.

96. Present interior of the Old Vic, London. Courtesy the Old Vic.

painted canvas covering in imitation of those sometimes used to shelter the audiences in Roman theatres. The Teatro Olimpico at Vicenza is thought to have at different times displayed both these treatments.

Much more commonly, however, the skies painted on these ceilings were peopled, sometimes with classical dramatists or scenes from their plays, but far more often with Apollo and the muses, often supported by additional figures representing comedy, tragedy, dance and music. The most common configuration simply showed Apollo arising in glory amid the clouds, but more discursive scenes were also offered, as in Galli Bibiena's design for the Imperial Theatre of Vienna in 1704, showing the sun god throwing the forces of darkness into the abyss, and Louis-Jacques Durameau's 1767 depiction on the Versailles court theatre ceiling of Apollo "crushing Ignorance and Envy" (Fig. 97).[11] Such subject matter not only reflected the almost universal conviction during the baroque period that the theatre should be an important source of moral and intellectual instruction, but at the same time celebrated the general baroque theme of the triumph of authority over rebel powers. Thus the triumphs of Apollo over the forces of ignorance and darkness on theatrical ceilings were closely allied to the pictorial triumphs of the sovereign over real and allegorical enemies in the galleries of the royal palace, or of the archangels or representations of Faith crushing rebellious powers in the decorations of baroque churches.

The development of monumental theatres in Europe beginning in the late eighteenth century changed both the locations and, to a lesser extent, the vocabulary of interior theatre decoration. The princely theatre had little need of foyers and similar auxiliary spaces, because the auditorium itself provided the setting for the display of the sponsoring prince. As the new theatres appeared, with an entire public seeking display space, the decorative grandeur that had previously been centered internally, around the royal box, now spread out into all sorts of entr'acte spaces—the foyers, galleries, and grand staircases so typical of the classic European opera house. The first architects of such spaces looked to princely dwellings for models, to royal salons and reception rooms and to grand galleries such as the hall of mirrors at Versailles (Fig. 98). The interior decoration traditionally associated with such spaces was copied also—the classical columns, the huge mirrors, the draperies, the gilded accents, the baroque statuary, and of course the painted ceilings.

These new monuments often reflected civic pride in their internal decoration just as they did in their external appearance and location, and local and municipal emblems appeared in the place of the royal and ducal emblems and attributes of an earlier time. The ceiling of the foyer of the Grand Théâtre de Bordeaux depicted that city as a new Athens, its modern palaces sheltering gods and muses while in the main auditorium a ceiling mural by one Robin, a local artist, cele-

[11]Dezallier d'Argenville *fils, Voyage pittoresque des environs de Paris* (Paris, 1779), 103.

97. The ceiling of the Versailles court theatre. Margarete Baur-Heinhold, *Theatre des Barock* (1966). Courtesy Verlag Callwey.

98. The grand foyer of the Paris Opéra. Courtesy Bibliothèque Nationale, Opéra.

brated the city's moral virtue by showing its opposition to slavery and its commercial success by including scenes of the wine industry.[12]

The allegorical auditorium ceilings of such painters as Durameau and Robin gave way at the end of the eighteenth century to more neutral and abstract designs, the old gods having fallen into disfavor through their unfortunate association with the aristocracy. Roman republicanism being now much in fashion, many theatre designers returned to the early Renaissance practice of painting ceilings to suggest the Roman *velum*. Sometimes a chaste color suggesting sailcloth was used, but the national theatre in Paris covered its muses with broad bands of red, white, and blue, while the Comédie Française offered geometric white and rose motifs on a green backing, colorful abstractions suggesting to contemporary audiences not so much the interior of a Roman theatre as that of a Montgolfier balloon.[13]

Such abstract compositions began to be replaced by the 1830s and 1840s with historical and allegorical subjects more suited to the nineteenth century's figurative pictorial taste. A French book on the "physiology of the theatre" in 1840 called interior decoration a matter of the utmost importance and insisted that "all the details of an auditorium ought to present to the eye the emblems of the specialty to which it is consecrated, and the attributes of the genre, the paintings testifying to its importance and to all that binds it to the nation and to humanity."[14] During the 1830s the painter Paul Joseph Chenavard proposed a complete redecoration of the interior of the Comédie Française, approved by the director, Baron Taylor, but never completed, which would have been the first elaborate working out of this new system. Bas-reliefs of early-seventeenth-century French farce players and of French classic tragedy were to frame the proscenium, with portraits of classic French dramatists above. Scenes from famous foreign plays were to decorate the box fronts and on the ceiling would appear a complex mural depicting the major Greek and Roman dramatists, Apollo, Minerva, Thespis, allegorical figures, and satyrs. The new decoration actually carried out during the 1840s by Pierre-Luc-Charles Ciceri and Nicolas-Louis-François Gosse was no less elaborate. Its outstanding feature was a vast allegory on the ceiling showing, at the highest point, the goddess Aurora ascending in a chariot. Beneath her was a sacred altar with the figures of Truth and Justice carrying a banner

[12]Pierre Vaisse, "Le décor peint dans le théâtre (1750–1900): Problèmes esthétiques et iconographiques," in *Victor Louis et le théâtre* (Paris, 1982), 165.

[13]Jean-Hughes Piettre, "Cent vingt-cinq ans de décorations . . . au Théâtre Français de la rue de Richelieu," unpublished, Archives of the Comédie Française, 43.

[14]Hippolyte Auger, *Physiologie du théâtre* (Paris, 1840), 92.

with a motto praising French genius and listing great names in French theatre history. Lower still were figures representing lyric, heroic, and satiric poetry as well as the allied arts of painting, sculpture, and architecture. Thalia and Melpomene were also shown exposing and rejecting figures representing the presumed targets of dramatic morality—Jealousy, Wrath, Despair, Avarice, Vanity, Perfidy, Envy, and Hypocrisy.[15]

This wholesale restoration of traditional mythological iconography in the "scientific" nineteenth century did not pass without protest from some critics and architects. "What a sad resource for modern art are these gods which have been a laughing stock for 2,000 years," lamented the *Revue générale d'architecture* when the Ciceri and Gosse work was unveiled. "Cannot something more original be discovered?"[16] When Adolphe Bouguereau painted the assembled gods of Olympus on the ceiling of the foyer at Bordeaux in 1869, the critic Jules-Antoine Castagnary reproached him for forgetting that the good citizens of Bordeaux were "not Greek shades but living beings, happy, busy, occupied, fond of their port, of their tree-lined boulevards, of their factories, justly proud of the beauty of their women and of the quality of their wines, intrigued by new liberal ideas, and strongly attached to the realities of everyday life."[17]

In some French theatres this sort of appeal to modern and local concerns was taken to heart. The foyer of the Toulouse theatre depicted views of the city and of the banks of the Garonne with strollers and laborers, and the 1889 foyer ceiling at Tours evoked, in allegorical form, the railway station, commerce, factories, and electric power as well as the surrounding châteaux of the Loire valley.[18] On the whole, however, theatres of the late nineteenth and early twentieth centuries offered less of this sort of local, commercial, and contemporary iconography than did other public buildings. The traditional pictorial vocabulary of Apollo, muses, and allegorical figures proved too strong to be easily dislodged. The Ciceri and Gosse ceiling was painted over in 1858, but only to be replaced by another vast allegory painted by F. J. Barrias. This was divided into four sections, one featuring Apollo and the muses, another depicting the origins of the drama, and one each devoted to tragedy and comedy and honoring the authors most celebrated in these genres from Greek times to the present.[19]

[15]Théophile Gautier, *Histoire de l'art dramatique*, 3 vols. (Leipzig, 1859), 2:152.
[16]*Revue générale d'architecture* 7 (1847), 315.
[17]Castagnary, *Salons* (Paris, 1892), 1:340.
[18]Vaisse, "Décor peint dans le théâtre," 163.
[19]Piettre, "Cent vingt-cinq ans," 94.

For the great monuments to nineteenth-century culture such as ornate national theatres and opera houses, this traditional vocabulary provided a kind of cultural authentication as important as the authentication of value provided by the equally ubiquitous chandeliers, pier mirrors, draperies, gold trimmings, and marble. In these secular cathedrals pagan gods, goddesses, and allegorical figures embellished every available space, as representations of the saints had done in the great baroque churches. The fullest development of this decorative concern, as of the nineteenth-century monumental tradition in general, may be seen in the Paris Opéra, where Garnier attempted to cover in the decoration the total vocabulary of classical emblem, ornament, and allegory. The elaborate decoration that had hitherto been concentrated in the auditorium was here extended to the many audience support spaces—the foyers, staircases, and galleries.

The decoration of all such spaces, like the auditorium, should, according to Garnier, suggest to the observer both the functions and the connotations of the theatre; a theatre "should have the character of a theatre, as a church has that of a church . . . the details as well as the whole should be related to the purpose of the monument," and this purpose involves "not only teaching, but also luxury and pleasure."[20] For those who complained that the building overworked such signs as masks, lyres, and figures of Apollo (one critic counted fifteen of these), Garnier responded with a rather strange historical argument—that all buildings eventually become ruins, and thus objects of study to future historians. Important public structures such as theatres must thus be clearly marked with signs of their use "to assure the accuracy of these future documents and make certain that our descendants, when they study our monuments, as we study those of the Greeks, are quite certain as to their purpose." The contemporary public is not forgotten, however. These, "surrounded by a rational atmosphere, feel themselves in homogeneous surroundings which work unconsciously on the spirit. Lyres and masks in theatres, like the crosses on altars, keep the thought oriented, by visual means, toward the central concern."[21]

Decorative symbols on a grand scale in the tradition of the great allegorical ceilings of the eighteenth and nineteenth centuries are still occasionally created for those theatres most closely associated with that tradition culturally, that is, monumental civic theatres, especially opera houses. Unquestionably the outstanding modern examples of this practice are Marc Chagall's creations during the 1960s first of a

[20]Charles Garnier, *Le théâtre* (Paris, 1871), 45.
[21]Garnier, *Le nouvel Opéra de Paris*, 2 vols. (Paris, 1870), 1:77.

new ceiling for the Paris Opéra, then of two giant murals for the grand
foyer of New York's Metropolitan Opera. These monumental works
are fascinating compilations of symbolic references to the artist, his
own work, his cultural heritage, and the decorative tradition to which
these works make a major contribution. The painter took "homage to
the Opéra's repertoire" as his unifying theme for the Paris ceiling.
Within its various sections, honoring major composers of opera and
ballet with motifs from key works, Chagall has returned to the nineteenth-century practice of placing the monumental ceiling visually by
depicting on it local physical landmarks. Thus a huge Eiffel Tower
separates Ravel from Stravinsky, Romeo and Juliet appear in the sky
(as Chagall lovers are wont to do) over the Place de la Concorde, the
Arc de Triomphe, and the Champs Elysées, and in the Rameau section
a huge angel bears a bouquet to the Opéra building itself. The style, the
composition, the coloring all mark this work as Chagall's, but he has
also included what are taken to be small figures of himself and his wife
before the Opéra and a great number of motifs so common in his
paintings as to serve as a kind of visual signature. Suitably, these
motifs, along with a self-portrait, are concentrated in the Stravinsky
section of the mural.[22]

Clearly the selection of Chagall to paint the ceiling of one of the
world's most famous opera houses had much to do with gaining him an
invitation from Rudolf Bing to create murals for the foyer of the new
Metropolitan Opera in Lincoln Center, and the Paris and New York
projects are closely related semiotically, not only in the general celebration of high culture they represent, but in the specific themes and
motifs Chagall employed. These two murals, called "The Sources of
Music" and "The Triumph of Music," are less specific in their references than the Opéra ceiling and have not been provided with the
small identifying titles the painter obligingly gave to many sections of
the Paris work. Chagall himself has provided a partial key to the paintings, but some identifications seem rather whimsical; some figures so
identified can scarcely be discerned, and some rather prominent figures
are not identified in the key at all.

"The Sources of Music" has the closer ties with the Opéra ceiling,
since it too is significantly concerned with signs of the repertoire and is
organized around a two-headed central figure, identified by the artist as
King David and Orpheus. As in Paris, city icons serve as referential
backgrounds for symbols of major composers and works. Romeo and

[22]Jacques Lassaigne, *Marc Chagall: The Ceiling of the Paris Opera*, trans. Brenda
Gilchrist (New York, 1966).

Juliet once again fly through the air, this time above the George Washington Bridge. Verdi's lovers embrace before a group of skyscrapers, with a skyline of Manhattan at night beneath their feet. The Hudson River, after passing under the bridge, runs in and out among the compositions on the right side of the mural until it flows past this night scene at the bottom.

"The Triumph of Music" is more abstract in its references, organized around a series of spirals containing small figures with trumpets called by the artist "The Song of the Peoples," with supplementary "homages" to American, Russian, and French music. In each corner of the composition and on the left side are views of New York—cityscapes and St. Patrick's Cathedral—and Chagall claims that a barely discernible shape on the left side of the mural is the head of Rudolf Bing. The artist and his wife appear next to a blue tree, and scattered across this mural and its companion are the usual Chagall angels, birds, floating violins, and other motifs.[23] The traditional celebrations of theatre, music, and the sponsoring city thus continue to inform these projects, but with the exception of Orpheus, himself blended into the cultural tradition of the artist, the conventional references of classical mythology have here been replaced by the personal, though widely recognized, mythology of Chagall.

The glass walls of the Met lobby allow strollers on the large square in front of the building to glimpse the Chagall murals, though they can be seen better from inside. According to the study *Chagall at the "Met,"* prepared by the Metropolitan Opera Society, the artist designed "The Triumph" to be placed on the north side, so that its angels would appear to be sending their music "out to the world." The more specific "Sources" was to be placed to the south, where its depictions of the opera house and its repertoire would relate more directly to the opera audiences. In the event, the positions of the murals were reversed. Chagall was at first horrified, but the diplomatic Bing convinced him that the angelic music of "Triumph" really more properly belonged to those lovers of music who patronized the Met than to the world outside, a semiotic coup d'etat to which Chagall was willing to agree.[24]

Even relatively modest public theatres from the eighteenth to the early twentieth century in Europe and North America tended to employ much the same decorative vocabulary of muses and lyres, laurel wreathes and putti, medallions and winged geniuses, all generally accepted to be the proper decoration for such spaces (Fig. 99). To this

[23]Emily Genauer, *Chagall at the "Met"* (New York, 1971), 30–33.
[24]Ibid., 46.

99. Boxes at the King's Theatre, Edinburgh. Photograph: Victor Glasstone.

general international vocabulary, of course, each cultural community added its own theatrical heroes in the form of statuary, busts, medallions, or inscribed names— Voltaire, Racine, Molière in France, Shakespeare, Garrick, Sheridan in England and the United States.

Fashionable English theatres of the nineteenth century most often looked to French decorative motifs from the previous century, then widely considered the ultimate expression of refined elegance. A London journal of 1841 remarked of the recently opened Princess's Theatre that it was "designed principally in the Louis Quatorze style—than which, for richness and relief, none is better adapted to the embellishment of theatres."[25] Louis XIV furnishings and decorations were then much favored in aristocratic English houses, and it was these elegant residences that now served, as the royal palaces had previously done, to provide models for the interior decoration of public theatres. Attending such a theatre remained, for many of its patrons, an opportunity to partake for a brief period of a world of high style which was normally beyond their reach (Fig. 100). A contemporary review of the remodeled St. James's Theatre in London in 1879 suggests the effect sought by such decoration: "The visitor, on entering, will imagine that he has passed the portals of some Parisian mansion, for the very ticket office has all the appearance of an antechamber sumptuously furnished— embossed green and gold wallpaper, a curiously carved walnut mantlepiece surmounted by a picture of Venus emerging from a shell and across from it the ticket box having all the appearance of an elegant cabinet with antique clock." Oriental rugs covered this lobby floor and a marble stairway led to upper lobbies with tapestried walls and mirrors, console tables and Venetian stools, and a picture gallery with ferns, fountains, "the Royal Academy on a small scale."[26]

As public ideas of fashionable elegance shifted, so did the decoration of such theatres. Even when the auditorium retained traditional motifs, one might find the architectural eclecticism of Victorian taste reflected (as they might also be in a wealthy residence) in an Indian entrance hall, a Japanese vestibule, a Moorish smoking room. For some years around the turn of the century, Louis XVI style, with colored marble walls, white, pink, and gold trimmings, and Rose du Barri hangings, was favored, to be replaced by a somewhat more restrained, though still elegant decorative style. Thus the *Architectural Review*

---

[25]*The Mirror of Literature, Amusement, and Instruction,* January 16, 1841, quoted in Raymond Mander and Joe Mitchenson, *The Lost Theatres of London* (New York, 1968), 337.

[26]*The Era,* October 5, 1879, quoted in Mander and Mitchenson, *Lost Theatres,* 468.

100. Interior public spaces at the Empire, London (opened 1884), during the 1890s. Victor Glasstone Theatre Architecture Collection.

commented in 1916 that London's recently opened St. Martin's Theatre reflected strikingly a change in decorative fashion "that has slowly been taking place during recent years. Its interior, instead of revelling in a lavish display of modelled plaster work, tricked out with gold leaf and paint, has an intimate, almost domestic character. In general style it tends to be what is known as English Georgian and gives one the impression of being a private theatre provided by some patron of the dramatic arts for the entertainment of his guests."[27]

The type of theatre interior recalling an eighteenth-century drawing room or salon, common in Europe at the turn of the century, may still be observed in the many theatres surviving from that period; occasionally more modern theatres, seeking to achieve an interior with a "traditional" feeling, still copy this style (Fig. 101). Thus London's New

[27]*Architectural Review* 40 (July–Dec. 1916), 132.

101. Lobby and box office of Her Majesty's Theatre (1897), London. Edwin O. Sachs and Ernest A. Woodrow, *Modern Opera Houses and Theatres*, 3 vols. (1896–98).

Royalty in 1960 boasted in its press release that its interior decoration was "designed to combine the dignity of the Georgian theatre and the lushness of the Victorian theatre in present-day terms."[28]

In general, however, these ornate turn-of-the-century decorative schemes were rarely seen after World War I. The costliness of their production was doubtless an important reason for their scarcity, but so was a change in decorative taste, reflected in such movements as art deco and modernism. Even as early as 1905 *The Builder* was complaining of the tradition according to which "a theatre interior seems to be considered only an opportunity for a kind of pie-crust decoration in a riot of plaster and gilding,"[29] and the simple, geometric interiors of such theatres as the Champs-Elysées (1913) in Paris or the Whitehall (1930) in London were warmly praised for their contemporary feeling. Changing ideas of the theatre as an art form and as a cultural object

[28]Raymond Mander and Joe Mitchenson, *Theatres of London* (New York, 1961), 162.
[29]*The Builder*, December 2, 1905, 1.

also contributed in important ways to the decline of traditional decoration, especially in the smaller, more experimental theatres that became so important a part of theatre culture in the new century.

The international art theatre movement of the early twentieth century was centrally concerned with freeing the theatre from commercial control and from its traditional ties to the privileged classes, and was well aware of the semiotic role played in this campaign by the tradition of internal theatre decoration, as may be clearly seen in Sheldon Cheney's 1917 book (revised 1925), *The Art Theatre.* Cheney characterizes traditional American theatre architecture as "pretentious, ornate, and vulgar imitations of showy French models," resulting from most architects' view of the theatre as primarily a "place of amusement designed to attract the money-spending public." The theatre in this tradition "reflected its commercial character in glitter, gaudiness and red-plush pretentiousness" as illustrated in "that culmination of the French-Italian social-democratic ideal, the ornate Paris Opera House."[30]

Cheney emphasized "simplicity and sobriety," and "absolute exclusion of distracting ornament and unmeaning detail" within the auditorium, in order to engender the sort of concentration and contemplative mood required for audiences in this temple of art (Fig. 102). This radical adjustment in the image of the proper decoration for a theatre auditorium reflects an equally radical change in the concept not only of what theatre ought to be, as Cheney suggests, but also of how it ought to be experienced. For most of the theatre's history, an important part of the event was the overtly social element in audience membership, and theatre structures (and auditoriums in particular) reflected this aspect by arranging for the proper display of the public to each other and for a suitably impressive setting for such display. During the late nineteenth century, this traditional aspect of the theatre experience came under severe attack, on the one hand from the realists and naturalists, who sought the illusion of real life on the stage and wished to remove, insofar as possible, the audience's consciousness of itself as audience, and on the other from artists such as Wagner, who wished his artistic creation to be the full focus of attention. These two approaches, doubtless reinforced by the functionalist and antidecorative emphasis of much modern architecture, cooperated to encourage the modern concept of the visually de-emphasized auditorium—minimally decorated, and totally darkened and thus invisible during the performance itself.

[30]Sheldon Cheney, *The Art Theatre* (New York, 1925), 253–54.

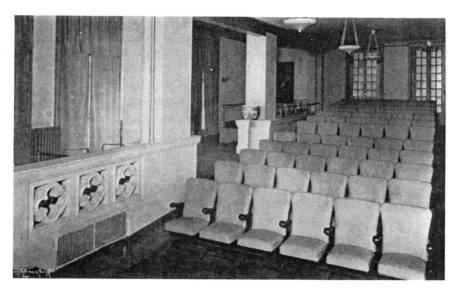

102. Interior of the Chicago Little Theatre. From Hiram Moderwell, *The Theatre of To-Day* (1914).

The lobbies and foyers of many modern theatres are thus more detailed in their decoration than the auditoriums, where the full attention of the audience is expected to be directed toward the stage. In the early twentieth century the allegorical emblems of dramatic art, the classical gods, and the cultural heroes tended to vanish from the auditorium and reappear in the now more visually elaborate lobbies and staircases. As more functionalist styles began to be fashionable and thus expected in such cultural spaces as theatre interiors, these traditional motifs tended to disappear from lobbies as well. Those still to be seen are either highly stylized or located in theatres whose interiors have been consciously preserved from an earlier era and which therefore display such elements with a kind of self-conscious historicity, as Molière's chair and the statue of Voltaire appear in the foyer of the Comédie Française. A feeling of luxury and elegance is still clearly sought in state-supported and large commercial theatres, but usually through the sweeping, simple lines and selected striking decorative elements of modern functionalism. The ostentatious statue of Shakespeare or bust of Molière is rarely to be seen—much more common is the discreet metal plaque acknowledging the contribution of some benefactor to the theatre.

The authenticating decor found in a modern lobby or foyer is much less likely to be sculpted or painted symbols of theatre art in general than a display of more temporary material concerning that specific theatre, its company, or even its current production. Posters, past and present, production and actor photographs, reproductions of reviews, may all frequently be found today in such spaces, especially, of course, in theatres established long enough to have accumulated an interesting number of such items to display. In some such theatres, as in today's Old Vic, this display is so extended as to give certain rooms and corridors the appearance of a small museum, encouraging audience members to situate themselves historically as well as culturally when attending a performance there.

The antagonism of theorists such as Cheney to traditional ornate theatre interiors acknowledged the semiotics of those interiors as objects for consumption and arenas for social display. Modern de-emphasized and darkened interiors and unadorned, utilitarian seating (as at London's Young Vic) owe much to such concerns. Other and more radical theorists of the early twentieth century plunged more deeply into the semiotics of theatre interiors and proposed changes much more sweeping than the eradication of "distracting ornament and unmeaning detail." Writers including Appia and Artaud, seeking to realize an entirely new vision of theatre, felt that even the basic traditional interior arrangements would work against any real reform. "Let us abandon these theatres to their dying past," wrote Appia, and erect instead simple buildings containing "no theatre, no stage, only a bare and empty room."[31] Similarly Artaud called for the abandonment of the "architecture of present-day theatres" in favor of "some hangar or barn, which we shall have reconstructed according to processes which have culminated in the architecture of certain churches or holy places. . . . The hall will be enclosed by four walls, without any kind of ornament, and the public will be seated in the middle of the room."[32]

The idea of such a neutral space, possessing no decorative features of its own and thus totally open to the semiotics of the individual performance, has been enormously influential in modern experimental theatre design, and the flexible "black box" has become one of the most common theatrical configurations of our time. Many later directors and designers have taken the characterless theatre in a direction quite different from the visions of Appia and Artaud, however. They have retained the concept of a space without the traditional auditorium and stage division, but instead of a featureless box filled by light and ab-

[31]Quoted in Simon Tidworth, *Theatres* (New York, 1973), 196.
[32]Antonin Artaud, *The Theatre and Its Double*, trans. Mary C. Richards (New York, 1958), 96.

stract figures, they have replaced the absent decoration (with all its evocations of a theatrical tradition) with a decoration unique to a specific production, so that the audience, entering the auditorium, is encompassed not within the semiotics of a theatre auditorium, but within those of the fictive world of the play itself. Thus, for example, in 1924 Max Reinhardt for one of the most famous of his productions, *The Miracle*, dazzled the theatre-goers of New York by converting the entire auditorium and stage of the Century Theatre into what appeared to be the interior of a vast Gothic cathedral, "not a mere contrivance of canvas and paint, but a solid structure of wood and iron and concrete and seeming stone,"[33] a feat repeated in several theatres in Europe. In the 1930s, for *The Iron Flood*, Nikolai Okhlopkov converted the entire interior of his Moscow theatre into a hillside where the audience sat among the actors as if "encamped with the Red Army in the field."[34] In the early 1960s Jerzy Grotowski in Poland converted his Laboratory Theatre space into a mental hospital for *Kordian*, with beds for patients and audience, and seated the audience for *Dr. Faustus* at long refectory tables as if they were guests for a banquet (Fig. 103).[35] "Environmental" performances of this type were introduced to the United States in 1967, when Ionesco's *Victims of Duty* was presented at the studio of Le Petit Théâtre du Vieux Carré in New Orleans. Here the entire auditorium and stage were "transformed into the living room of the play's principal characters—a room which, during the performance, was inhabited not only by the actors but by the audience as well."[36] Peter Stein's *As You Like It* (1977) brought his audience into a "complete woodland environment" for the Forest of Arden, with recorded birdsong, a pond, real trees, a field of corn, and acting areas scattered among the audience.[37] An even more extreme form of such "environmental" theatre has been the production of *Tamara*, by John Krizanc, offered first in Toronto in 1981 and subsequently in Los Angeles and New York. For this production, ten large rooms are furnished to represent Il Vittoriale, the country villa of Gabriele D'Annunzio, in 1927, and audience members follow any one of the play's actors through these rooms during the evening, thus experiencing only that part of the total action in which that character is involved.

We have in these examples a phenomenon clearly related to the use

[33]"Scenic Miracle Wrought," *New York Times*, January 16, 1924, p. 17.

[34]Norris Houghton, *Moscow Rehearsals* (New York, 1936), 23.

[35]Jennifer Kumiega, *The Theatre of Grotowski* (New York, 1985), 56, 67–68.

[36]Brooks McNamara, Jerry Rojo, Richard Schechner, *Theatres, Spaces, Environments* (New York, 1975), 2.

[37]Michael Patterson, *Peter Stein* (Cambridge, 1981), 139.

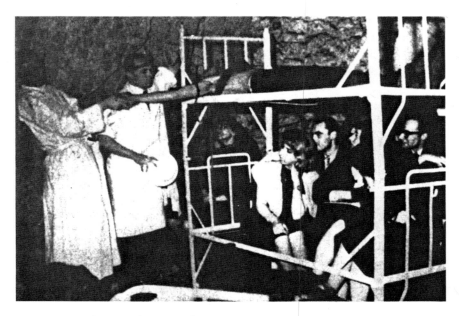

103. Grotowski's production of *Kordian*. From *Towards a Poor Theatre* by Jerzy Grotowski. Copyright © 1968 by Jerzy Grotowski and Odin Teatrets Forlag.

of spaces outside the theatre for theatrical performance discussed earlier, but the creation and the reception of the sign are working in a rather different way. Edward William Godwin's *As You Like It* converted an actual woods into a sign for the Forest of Arden by staging the Pastoral Players' production within it. Stein converted a stage/auditorium space into such a sign by bringing synecdochic elements of the forest (the almost invariable practice in such experiments) into his theatre and then staging the play among them. Reinhardt converted theatre interiors into icons of cathedral interiors, but he also made plans, unrealized, to stage his *Miracle* in the actual cathedral in Milan. Many of the connotations of the decor surrounding both performers and spectators would not have been affected by such a change, but certainly others would have. The actual object, though standing for another, absent space, nevertheless carries with it inescapably some of the connotations of its embedding in reality and history, and these will necessarily condition the audience response. The created interior, even utilizing real objects and authentic materials, is framed in a different way by an audience. Part of its connotations necessarily recognizes its artifice, and part of the audience response and pleasure is based on this recognition.

104. A production of Mozart's *Bastien and Bastienne* at the Drottningholm theatre in Sweden. Photo: Lennart af Petersens.

Finally, even the traditional theatre interior itself and its decor can be and has been opened to a process of reflexive iconicity. When summer tourists attend the court theatre at Drottningholm in Sweden, they are welcomed by ushers in eighteenth-century costume and witness a similarly costumed and wigged orchestra accompanying what seems to be a period performance of a Mozart opera (Fig. 104). This whole sign complex is held together by the semiotic of the theatre auditorium, an actual eighteenth-century structure with its original decor intact. When *The Phantom of the Opera* came from London to the Majestic Theatre in New York, part of the $1.5 million spent in remodeling the theatre to accommodate it went toward changing the entire physical cadre. "All the details are really important," noted director Hal Prince, "because an audience has to believe they are inside the opera house. We even built Victorian gaslights outside. You have to look at the theatre's whole environment—the exterior, the lobby. . . . We're going into a theatre to see a piece about this theatre, a piece that takes you back 110 years."[38]

The theatrical self-consciousness of a play such as Pirandello's *Tonight We Improvise* or *The Phantom of the Opera* requires that we foreground the awareness that we are in fact in a theatre, and in such situations traditional auditorium decor, far from distracting from the performance, provides an essential semiotic support for it. From this point, additional connotative levels develop naturally. The theatre interior, established as an icon of itself, becomes open to further signification based on the cultural meanings of that interior. A recent production of Brecht's *Mahagonny* at the lavishly decorated Theater des Westens in Berlin, traditionally a home for operetta and musical comedy, called attention to the gilt and crystal opulence of the theatre's interior by such devices as putting blindfolds on the putti flying about the stage, thus allowing Brecht's parable on capitalism and consumption to be framed dialectically by a theatre interior embodying the very values under attack.

A far more complex example of this kind of ironic self-reference may be seen at the Bouffes du Nord in Paris. Director Peter Brook has kept the interior decoration of this theatre essentially as he found it: the traditional late-nineteenth-century elaborate decor fallen into decay during the long abandonment of the theatre. It has been characterized as a "real space" simultaneously architecture and scenography, "a structure beyond the suspicion of forced illusion,"[39] but its "reality" is hardly devoid of signification. In Brook's *Ubu* the stained and peeling walls of this long-abandoned theatre seemed to place the audience in a decaying world highly suited to Alfred Jarry's apocalyptic farce. In the era of post-structuralism, one is tempted to see in the fading colors and crumbling plasterwork of the Bouffes du Nord the decor of a theatre "under erasure," where Brook pursues his experiments at the frontiers of theatrical possiblity. The simultaneous affirmation and denial of the decoration here allows a rich play of signification and suggests some of the many ironic possibilities opened by a consciousness of the contri-

[38]Quoted in Patricia Morrisroe, "Here Comes the Phantom," *New York*, January 18, 1988, 32.

[39]Georges Banu, "Landscape Painting with Variations in French Scenography," *The Drama Review* 28 (Summer 1984), 40.

bution of interior decoration to the theatre's image and the audience's experience.

Further connotative levels beyond the "traces" of decoration in the Bouffes du Nord might seem unlikely, but only to those unfamiliar with the vertiginous possibilities of the semiotic process. When Brook brought his *Mahabharata* to New York, his venue was another Majestic Theatre, this one in Brooklyn, which, like the Bouffes du Nord, has been abandoned and allowed to decay for more than twenty years. Its five-million-dollar remodeling made no attempt to restore it to its original 1903 appearance, but rather turned it into an architectural icon of the present Bouffes du Nord (Fig. 105). "The challenge was to create the appearance of an old theatre in a state of decay," said Evan Carzis, the architect, and indeed the details of the interior were carefully supervised not only by Brook but by his scenic designer and technical director from the Bouffes. The scenic designer, Chloe Obolensky, even found it necessary to paint holes and cracks in the lobby walls to give a properly "aged" appearance.[40]

Architectural critic Michael Kimmelman has posited a relationship between the remodeling of the Brooklyn Majestic and the strong historicizing tendencies that have dominated architecture since the late 1960s, which lead to decorative elements from the past being employed with an "artificial impasto of time laid across the entire design." He sees a connection between the present Brooklyn Majestic and "the follies that British aristocrats built on the hills of their country estates roughly two centuries ago."[41] There is likely some truth in this, but it is only a small part of the semiotic story. The Majestic's most important reference is not synecdochically to past glories of theatre architecture nor metonymically to decay and romantic ruins, but iconically to the Bouffes du Nord, and it seeks to evoke the connotations of avant-gardism and experimentation now internationally associated with that physical structure.

There is thus an important semiotic link between the apparently quite different remodelings of New York's two Majestic theatres in 1987. The Broadway Majestic, in order to house a costly, highly technological musical spectacle, has been converted into an icon of the Paris Opéra, the theatre that socially and historically most embodied the high bourgeois aesthetic of which *The Phantom of the Opera* is a

[40]Susan Heller Anderson, "Restoring a Theater to Its Decrepit State," *New York Times*, December 13, 1987, 84.
[41]Michael Kimmelman, "Putting Old Wrinkles into a Theater's New Face," *New York Times*, October 25, 1987, 41.

105. The Majestic Theatre, Brooklyn. Photo by David J. Epstein.

central contemporary example. The Brooklyn Majestic, in order to house what is generally considered the decade's central example of experimental theatre, and moreover an experimental theatre that has specifically disavowed the elegance and technological prowess of the major commercial stage, has been converted into an icon of a very different Parisian theatre, devoted to and particularly associated with that counteraesthetic. And finally, to hark back to an earlier concern in this book, I must remark that the physical locations of these two new icons within New York's urban text are perfectly selected to reinforce these connotative concerns.

Conclusion

Among the characteristics claimed for their works by some of the creators of the experimental performances styled "happenings" during the 1960s was that their actions were "nonmatrixed"—that is to say, these actions were performed simply for what they were, without the conventional theatrical matrices of time, place, and character. An actress burning papers was simply performing that action, rather than assuming the role of Hedda Gabler burning Lovberg's manuscript in the stove of her Norwegian home in the 1890s.

This distinction, though undeniably useful in indicating one important difference between an event such as a happening and a conventional theatrical performance, nevertheless continues to direct our attention, as theoretical considerations of traditional performance also almost invariably do, to the internal characteristics of that performance. If we look at the performance event in a more global sense, as it is actually created and experienced within a culture, we realize that all performance is invariably matrixed, and that the matrices of the event are enormously influential in conditioning our reception of that event. Among other things, it is the matrix that informs us whether a particular action is to be understood as a happening or as a more conventional theatrical scene.

The investigations in this book have sought to suggest that in every historical period and in every culture the physical matrices of the theatrical event—where it takes place within the community, what sort of structure houses it, and how that structure is organized and decorated—all contribute in important ways to the cultural processing of the event and must be taken into consideration by anyone seeking to gain an understanding of its dynamics. The examples used have come largely from the tradition of Western theatre, with which I am most familiar, but there is little doubt that the analysis of spatial semiotics and of the semiotics of decoration could be applied to non-Western theatres as well for similar insights into the messages these provide for their audiences.

Although all situations involving the performance of theatre begin with the same basic dialectic—a confrontation of the observer and the observed—the historical variations upon this basic theme have been almost infinitely varied, allowing the physical organization, location, and ornamentation of the theatrical space to provide for a vast variety of messages relevant to the cultural concerns of those who utilize it. Theatres have been designed to accommodate entire communities or single spectators, to surround their audience with Spartan simplicity or with the greatest luxury the society could afford, to stress the essential equality of all audience members or to reflect in astonishing detail the most subtle differences in social status. Theatres have been located in the commercial centers of cities, in the most elegant residential areas, in working-class neighborhoods, and in the most disreputable and socially marginal situations. They have been highly prominent city landmarks and clandestine hideaways whose location was known only to a few initiates. They have been designed as temples of art, seeking to remove their audiences from the concerns or even any visual echoes of everyday life, and they have been created out of the very texture of that life, out of the raw material of streets, marketplaces, and factories, foregrounding for spectators the nontheatrical cultural associations of these locations.

The conscious awareness of theatre audiences of the specific semiotics of their performance surroundings has naturally varied at different times and in different places, but on the whole, audiences have surely been conscious to a considerable degree of the connotations of these surroundings, even when their significance has not been a common theme in contemporary records of performance. The relative merits of each box in an eighteenth-century opera house was absolutely essential social information to its patrons. The type of interior decoration, its lavishness, and its style will clearly contribute greatly to determining whether an audience member feels comfortable or out of place in a particular theatre. City dwellers have always known, with considerable agreement and often in surprising detail, the social semiotics of different sections of their city, and it is inevitable that this coding will affect their attitudes toward the locations of theatres. Culturally we learn to read the messages of theatre spaces, locations, and decoration just as we do the many related architectural and urban codes by means of which we intellectually structure our environment. In the ordinary theatrical experience, the performance itself is foregrounded as the highly complex object presented for our reception, and this foregrounding often encourages a kind of bracketing of the rest of the event structure in analysis of the experience. It is clear, however, that the physical surroundings of performance never act as a totally neutral filter or frame. They are themselves always culturally encoded, and have always, sometimes blatantly, sometimes subtly, contributed to the reception of the performance. The student of theatre who seeks to understand the public presentation of a play without some knowledge of this performance matrix will inevitably be dealing with a partial perspective and in many cases with a seriously flawed one.

A few final comments might be made on the particular dimensions of this type of investigation as it may be applied to the modern theatre, an area of particular complexity. Two often-noted characteristics of the modern consciousness—its eclecticism and its reflexivity—have major implications for modern practices in and thus cultural understanding of performance space. Never before in history has a public had available for its consideration paintings, music, or drama from so wide a range of cultures and historical periods. The same eclecticism characterizes the physical spaces in which theatre today may be presented. A certain cultural image of the "standard" theatre structure still exists. For many persons in our society this image is of the nineteenth-century facade structure, especially as found today in New York, London, or Paris. For others, especially in Germany or in those cities in England, France, or North America where the regional theatre movement has made an impact, the image may well be that of the free-standing monument of eighteenth-century urban planning, executed in accordance with contemporary architectural taste.

As the examples in this book have suggested, however, our modern culture offers a vast variety of other, less widely coded models for performance spaces. Nineteenth-century historicism encouraged the revival of historic theatre spaces, and we may today, unlike theatregoers in any previous period, experience theatre in almost every type of historical space. Actual theatres from other periods have been used for performance, and modern reconstructions of theatre structures no longer in existence have been attempted. Passion plays in Oberammergau, in South Dakota, and in Arkansas regularly offer huge spectacles on multiple stages in the manner of a medieval location like Valenciennes. Pageant wagons may be seen in the streets of York in England and Toronto in Canada. Greek tragedies are staged in the ruins of actual Greek theatres and in smaller-scale copies of them on American college campuses. A permanent commedia dell'arte theatre is featured in Copenhagen's Tivoli Gardens. Baroque operas are presented in court theatres still existing from that era. Shakespeare's Globe has been reconstructed in a variety of versions in North America, and plans have been made to reconstruct it again near its original location in London.

A variety of motives lies behind these experiments. Historians seek to gain understanding of historical performance by approximating its physical conditions. Entrepreneurs try to attract a public by playing upon a touristic interest in new and "authentic" experiences from other times and cultures. Communities aim to continue or to revive local pride or self-knowledge by recreating performance in a matrix selected or designed to reinforce such concerns. Whatever their motives, these offerings allow a modern spectator willing to undertake a certain amount of travel to attend performances that at least approximate the physical situation of theatre in almost every historical period.

In addition to this huge selection of historical spaces, the twentieth century has produced experimental directors who have explored the possibilities of an almost infinite variety of nontraditional spaces as well. Theatre has been seen in the streets, in parks and woodlands, in factories and warehouses, and in all manner of public and private buildings. Here again many different motives lead to such exploration. An abandoned factory may be chosen as a performance space for aesthetic reasons—because it provides an "authentic" background for a play set in a factory, or because a director or designer is intrigued by the particular spaces it offers—or for economic reasons—because a producing organization finds that utilizing such a space is far less expensive than building a traditional theatre—or for political reasons—because a director such as Gatti may sense an aura of the departed workers still existing in such a space, making a production there more accessible to a working-class audience than one in a conventional theatre. Each approach will take a somewhat different attitude toward the balance in this "found" space between the semiotics it already possesses in its previous role and those that might be imposed upon it as it is used for performance.

This vast array of possibilities in performance spaces has clearly heightened the awareness of producers of performance concerning the semiotic potential of such spaces, and only an audience member of very limited experience today is likely to be unaware that the framing of the theatre experience has become a calculated part of that experience. In this way the theoretical self-consciousness so typical of modern art in all its aspects has entered this area of the theatre experience. In all earlier periods there was a certain awareness of the signifying potential of performance surroundings, but the rather narrow range of possibilities explored in each era tended to limit both speculation about and experiment with such potential. The modern interest in both the dynamics of historical performance and in the semiotic potential of nontraditional spaces works to foreground the matrix of the performance experience. By bringing to our consciousness this vital element in modern performance, that interest may also encourage us to see the importance of matrix in other eras, since our traditional emphasis upon the dramatic text, both written and performed, has often led us to neglect the other conditioning elements of the theatre event.

Index